Pig:

You are here for A Reason, God Has Plans for You.

An autobiography
By Leroy "Pig" Jackson

Edited by
Leroy Jackson
Michelle Herrin

Leroy "Pig" Jacskson 2178624896
michelleherrin@ymail.com
leroypigjackson@yahoo.com
Please note: This work is registered with the U.S. copyrights office.

Table of Content

Acknowledgements..7

Black men..8

Introduction...10

Glossary...12

Chapter 1..17

The Beginning 18

Poor..25

I thought stuff like this only happened on

TV..26

Sex for payment...30

Double Jugging..33

Karma...35

Back to Grandma's..40

Do not disturb..43

Shit Happens..44

Am I my brother's keeper? Yes I am....................................45

Chapter 2..55

My first Jab...56

My Move with my Auntie...57

Graduating in the upstairs neighbors Air

Force One's……………………………………………………..60

My Mama Came Home……………………………………..64

Chapter 3…………………………………………………...**69**

My Move to Springfield………………………………………..70

The Team………………………………………………….73

The First time I met Bethany……………………………….80

Highway Robbery…………………………………………81

Tupac's Back……………………………………………..83

Stick Bandit………………………………………………86

Juvie Stint………………………………………………...90

For the Love of Guns……………………………………...93

Snitches Get Stitches………………………………………96

Brah's Side Chick/ Our Chick……………………………..97

Indictments………………………………………………101

Surprise…………………………………………………..107

We at War Over Here, Homie…………………………...108

Fireman/You Gotta Move Tonight……………………....113

Choked out……………………………………………....118

3 Balls…………………………………………………...120

Chaos: Disorganized…………………………………….122

Vol II

Chapter 4

That's Not My Shit, Man

Just Say "Yes"

Boot camp

The only thing boot camp changed about me was my attitude; my hustle got stronger!

My Old School

If you run Me Over: I'm Gon' Shoot Yo' Ass

Speaker Phone

All I heard was A Loud Boom

My First Connect

The Rats Smelled Cheese

Chapter 5

I am Knocking her Down too

Disrespectful Bitch

Flashback

Get out of town

Brah, hurry up and get Home

You Mean to Tell Me This Isn't you

Binoculars

Taking Turns

Bingo

There is No Way in Hell that my little Brother should've Fucked Up

Chapter 6

Turn it Down, Turn it Down

Shackles and Chains

Bathroom Break

Letting it Soak Dry

The Big Sit Down

This is Hell for Me

Out and Facing 9

Bang, Bang, Bang

It was real cool…At First

Bait and Switch

Chapter 7

Can't Turn a Hoe into a Hood wife but I tried

Dreaming

Yoke

Middle Man's Middle Man

ATF

Bitch I Need My Money

Ol' Snitch Bitch

College Hoes, Hood Rats, and Lies

Uncut

New Beginning

Bibliography

Acknowledgements

I would not have been able to write this book if it was not for the love of my life, Michelle Herrin. Honestly, I do not know where I would have ended up in life; if it were not for my family; my grandmother, Margret Jackson, my auntie, Margret Walson, and my Uncle, Riley Walson. They took me in when I had nowhere else to go. Throughout all the bad times in my life, I have always had my two brothers; Eugene Jackson and Donnell Jackson. I would like to give thanks to God. I am thankful for waking up in the right state of mind every single day with my family and a roof over my head. Last but not least I would like to thank my parents; Karen Jackson and Leroy Gaston; if it wasn't for them I would not be here.

Black men

I am a black man from Chicago Illinois. Right now, there is a war in Chicago. Black men deal with drugs, mass incarceration, and violence. These three factors break up the structure of black families. I have been a victim/participant in all three areas. I hope this book can bring more light to the problem and solution. Here are some statics of what black men are currently dealing with, in regards to the chance of being arrested in America:

Lifetime Likelihood of Imprisonment

Source: Bonczar, T. (2003). *Prevalence of Imprisonment in the U.S. Population, 1974-2001*. Washington, D.C.: Bureau of Justice Statistics.

All people do bad things and make mistakes, but when the police are sitting and waiting for black people to mess up, it makes a big difference on the arrest rates. Black men need to take their power back and live their lives with purpose—find a dream and chase it.

Introduction

Hi, my name is Leroy Jackson, but everyone calls me Pig. It has been my nickname since I was a baby. I was born; weighing 13 lbs. in Chicago Illinois at Bethany hospital on May 5th 1986. I wrote this book because I learned that I have a story to tell. About a year ago, my lady was sitting down doing her homework and I started telling her stories about my childhood. She stopped doing her homework, and made me tell her my entire life story. I told her "since you like my stories so much I'm going to write a book" So, she inspired me to write this book.

When I began writing the book, I was not sure what to do. I bought a composition notebook and began writing by hand. I soon realized that was going to take 134 years to complete. I then began writing on my phone. It took me under a year to get it all done. My whole reason to push this book is to get America reading. I want people to put down the garbage in their lives and pick up a book. I want to encourage everyone to read books every day. The first time I read an entire book; I was 27 years old. I now read books every day. My goal is for my book to get teenagers reading, writing, and telling their stories. I am pushing for a reading America!

I want to help someone out there that is just like me. My two brothers and I grew up poor, on the west side of Chicago, raising ourselves. That is what is wrong with most of the black community in Chicago; once kids reach a certain age; their parents leave them to fend for themselves. I am not putting every family in this category but something is clearly wrong with family structure in Chicago today. Families break up for many reasons, but let's think about some specific things; drugs and jail.

It is going to be some things in this book that are going to be hard for you to understand but as Ralph Waldo Emerson would say, "Treat a man as he is, and he will remain as he is. Treat a man as he could be, and he will become what he should be."

Glossary

Backyard Boogie - A very low grade of weed.

Balls (8 Ball, Borskey) – 100 worth of cocaine. It depends on the drought but it can be anywhere from 1.7-3.5 grams.

Bench Marks- Muscles

Blanket Party- To throw a blanket over someone's head and beat their ass.

Blow- Heroin, that boy.

Brick (Book, Key) – 36 ounces of cocaine.

Buddy (lil or little Buddy) – A term used to describe someone that is a straight creep.

Clucks - A person that smoke's crack.

Double Jugging - working for two drug dealers on one drug dealers spot.

XIV

Double Up- Selling someone crack for a two for one special.

Front Street- putting someone/thing out there for everyone to see.

Get it off - Sell drugs.

Jabs- 25 bags of $5 cocaine.

Juicin'- Having sex.

Lock it up – Cooking crack and it hardens up.

On Site- Instantly as soon as the chance is available.

Quarter (Quad) – 7 grams of cocaine.

Recop- Buy more drugs.

Serves- Making drug deals.

The Brother's (Moe's) - Black Peace Stones.

Work (White Girl) – Crack.

Zip - An ounce of cocaine.

Pig:

You are here for A Reason, God Has Plans for You.

1

"And this too shall pass away" -Abraham Lincoln

"Mother fucker you crazy, You gon' put yo' hands on me?"

-Karen Jackson

The Beginning

One common question we all have is "what is the point of life" I have spent years wondering what is my purpose. Was I just put here to live and die? Was I born to be a hustler? Was I put here to take care of my family? These things are all true. I also found out that I am here to touch as many lives as I can and leave my mark. For me to gain a better understanding on this thing we call life. I took it all the way back. I have made a lot of mistakes and I can honestly say I am a better man for it. The crack epidemic affected a lot of families, mine included. Back in Chicago, in the late 80's a majority of my aunts and uncles were selling crack, and smoking it. My parents were also affected by the epidemic. My mom was a hustler. I learned a lot from her.

    Looking back on my life; I have done a lot of fucked up shit. As far back as I can remember, really. I never had much growing up, but one thing I always had was my brothers. There are three of us; my older brother, Eugene, I call him Brah, he also goes by Huggie, he is three years older than me. Then, there is me, I go by Pig. And lastly, my little brother Donnell, he is one year younger than me. People usually do not remember where it goes bad for them in their life, but I can give you an exact age, age two. I was jealous that my mom had another baby, so I use to pick my little brother up and hide him under her bed. Two years later, on Christmas, I remember my mom and pops sitting in the room talking about how bad I was. They were asking each other what could possibly be wrong with me. They gave both of my brothers their presents and told me Santa did not bring anything for me, because I was so bad. I went back in my room, cried, and went to sleep. Later, they woke me up and took me into the kitchen. They pulled my present's out of the cabinets, and they told me that Santa was not coming next year if I was still bad. That next year I was jealous of my big brother; he got a power wheel for Christmas. So, I went into the closet and I ripped all of the cords out of it. I was always getting into fights with my brothers. One time I took a toy from Brah; he cracked me in the forehead with a curtain rod and I had to get stitches. To this day, I have this football stitch shaped scar on my forehead.

One day after school, my mom put an S curl perm in my hair. I guess, she looked at the time and realized that Brah should have been home from school by now; she thought he was outside playing. She told me "go downstairs and get Eugene so he can get his damn hair done". As I walked outside, I saw Brah surrounded by four or five people. They were pushing him around. We grew up around "4 corner hustlers". Because my pops was a Blackstone, Brah would always tell people he was a Blackstone. Those 4 corner hustlers were about to fuck him up. I walked over to them and told Brah "mom said, "get your ass upstairs and get your hair done"". The 4's turned to me and I thought they were about to kick both of our asses, instead they all started rubbing on my hair "damn shorty that's nice, who did that to your head" I told them "my mom just put an S curl in my hair" as Brah took off running. My S curl saved him from getting an ass whooping that day.

Growing up in the projects was crazy. The first time I had sex, I was 6 years old. We called it Juicin'. It was with the girls down the hall, at the neighbor's house, and it was a fucked up incident. What happened was, my mom's friend, whom had three daughters, was raped by a person that everyone in the hood called "Cow Boy" because he always wore a cowboy hat. As the story goes, "Cow Boy" cut her pussy lips off and put them in a jar. She was at the hospital for a week. My mom watched her daughters. I remember it like it was yesterday. I woke up, in the middle of the night; I had to use the bathroom. Both of my brothers were having sex with one of the girls. The girl told me to get on top of her. I got on top of her, but I still had to use the bathroom and she told me to pee in her and I did.

My brothers and I had fun growing up in the projects. I know most people have a sad story and hate that they lived there, but we had many good times. There was this one time, I helped save a baby. There was a shoot-out at the project's playground and the mother (of the baby) took off running and left her baby in the swing. She stood there crying out "my baby, my baby". I ran back out to the swing and got the baby. (These are just bits and pieces that I remember from growing up) Throughout my childhood, we would move back and forth into my grandma's house. My grandma had 12 kids and five of them lived on their own; the rest of them lived with her. As I got older, I realized my mom had pride issues and would rather be in the streets than stay at my grandma's house. We had to go with my mom and stay in shelters and in and out of her different boyfriend's houses. I liked staying with my grandma, but she was a crazy old bat. She had all kinds of weapons in the corner by the front door. She had an ass whooping station set up. She had bats, sticks, poles, and police car atenas— you know the long ones (where the fuck did she even get that from?) But, the bad thing about staying with her was, she would get drunk. We would all be sleeping, it didn't matter what time it was and she would wake us up by punching us and yelling "get up and go find your God damn mama". My grandma had a big ass house with six bedrooms. We use to have to fight my uncles for our bedrooms, when they would get out of jail. They would get out and expect to have the same bedroom they had before they went to jail. When my uncles would get locked up; we'd move into the big rooms. When my uncle Wayne got out of

Jackson   *Pig: you are here for a reason, God has plans fo[r]*

jail, he saw my mom, my two brothers, and I were staying in hi[s]
wanted it back. Uncle Wayne and my mom got into an argumen[t]
her in the stomach causing her to have an asthma attack. We jum[ped]
we had to whoop his ass. We ended up getting to keep the room. My uncle was fresh out of jail, so he had to get back to the hustle. His main grind was fixing cars, but he also sold drugs on the side. One day, we looked outside and saw my Uncle Wayne wrestling with this dude, in front of the house. At first, we thought they were kidding around, but as it turns out, the guy was trying to rob him and he shot my uncle in the leg. Shortly after, he had an incident with the police; causing them to chase him into the house. He ran into our room and an officer tackled him. They cuffed him and then proceeded to search the house. While they were searching, they left him unattended. He said to me "reach under my balls, boy, and grab this Jab"

I went into his pants, grabbed the Jab and hid it under my pillow. They arrested him and took him to jail. When they left, I gave it to my mom. Only the lord knows what she did with it. He got out that morning. I saved him from that case.

    Living at my grandma's house was so crazy. Let me ask you something, have you ever gotten a wet, bloody, naked ass whooping? Well let me explain: One day my little brother and I were playing in the tub. My grandma had a big French style tub. (We liked to wet the edges of the tub and slide around it as if we were on a staircase banister) On this particular day, my mom kept yelling to us "y'all keep getting water down here on the floor. Y'all need to stop playing around in the tub. If I have to tell you again; I am coming to whoop y'all ass" That's what gave me the idea to lather it with soap instead ater, so we would not get our asses whooped. I sat on the edge of the tub and took my swing around. The shit was so slippery; I almost went thru the wall. I fell and cut my back on the faucet. I fell in the water "splash" water went everywhere! The whole tub was bloody. My little brother jumped out and yelled

"mom, mom, he's bleeding"

She came in yelling

"Didn't I tell y'all to stop playing in this Goddam tub. Now all of downstairs is wet up. Now you're all bloody and I gotta take you to the hospital"

Black moms always say

"now I gotta take you to the hospital"

But, I never went. I never went for any of my injuries.

That's when she came in and walled on my ass. And that is the meaning of a wet, bloody, naked ass whooping.

    Whenever my mom would just leave us; my grandma would get mad and tell us we had to get out at two or three in the morning. We would have to go sleep on the porch. We had cousins that stayed three houses down and they would see us sleeping outside and let us come sleep at their house. But, that was never fun; we never had shit and they use to talk about us. Whenever we would fall asleep, they would put mustard and ketchup on us. The next day, we would have to go to school wearing the same clothes, day after day, with mustard and ketchup on them. I remember one time sitting at my desk and another student asking me "Pig, what is that yellow stuff in your hair" I reached up and scrapped dried mustard out of my hair. I remember being at school and feeling how sticky I was from all of the syrup, they had poured on us while we were sleeping. One night I fell asleep in the basement and I woke up with a part of my shirt on fire from where they dropped a lit match on me. I did not like staying there but what else could we do. My grandma had this big sectional on her porch and we would cuddle up on that and fall asleep. Kids at school would talk about us and we would get into fights because we would stink and wear the same clothes for days. We would always fight our cousins (the same ones that would let us stay the night) every summer. Ron was my oldest cousin and he would always start the fights with us. This one summer, Ron tried to show off in front of the neighbor girls. He walked up and clothes lined me off the girl's porch. I could not find Brah, so I went and told my dad about it. My dad and I walked back to Ron's house together. I picked up a stick and my dad told me "you better whack his ass with it" He saw me coming towards him so he walked up to me. I whacked him in the head--like three or four times. That is when both of our brothers (Brah and his little brother) popped up. We all started fighting. Ron had this motto "if you can't beat 'em bite 'em"

He could not handle my haymakers. I was beating his Ol' tall goofy ass. He grabbed my arm and bit a plug out of it (I still have the scar, you can see the teeth prints to this day) And I didn't go the hospital for that either. I ran on my grandmas porch screaming; blood shooting out everywhere! I think he bit a vain. My little brother came out of nowhere and busted a 40 oz. across his face. It cut his face up badly; he had a black eye for weeks. That boys face was fucked up for the whole summer. I don't even think he went to the hospital. Growing up at my grandma's house, all of my aunts, uncles, and even my mom smoked crack. Sometimes we would walk in the room and see them smoking the pipe. While I was with my mom, we would stay with whatever man she was with at the time or at homeless shelters. The first guy's house I remember staying with was in a basement, I can't remember his name. I just remember the basement and how fucked up it was. It was just my little brother and I, staying with her at the time. My big brother was staying at my grandma's house. I remember one night I couldn't sleep because the guy (we were staying with) was messing with my mom. I just remember her saying

"stop, stop, stop leave me alone, you just gonna rape me in front of my kids?"

I was to young at the time to understand that I should've done something. I just rolled over and went to sleep feeling mad. To this day, I have not told her. Then we went to stay at my grandma's house, and my mom stayed there for a couple days. Then she went back to the streets. We stayed there until my grandma was tired of us. She would kick us out and yell for us to go find our mom and whatever guy she was staying with. Then my mom and the guy would get into a fight and we'd go back to a shelter. Going from place to place, we missed out on a lot of schooling.

Poor

Growing up in the house was crazy: fighting my uncles for a room to sleep in, watching them fight each other, watching them smoke crack, and going without eating. What do you know about eating syrup sandwiches, mayonnaise sandwiches, sugar sandwiches and ketchup sandwiches? I went thru it growing up. We ended up moving in with my mom's boyfriend Trish. It was a big house. He lived with his mom and my mom took care of her. We stayed in the attic. Trish had a nephew that stayed there. Trish's sister would bring her three daughters over while she went to work. She had a set of twins and an older daughter. The older daughter and I were playing house one day and we were caught, touching each other. Trish told her mom. Her mom said "I am going to cut that little mother fuckers dick off" She said "mommy no don't do that" We all ended up moving down into the basement. I remember playing hide and go seek with my little brother. A little while later, his nephew came down stairs and got in the bed with me. He molested me. He told me not to tell anybody. I never did until now. That night I went to sleep and I was in the top bunk. I woke up in my mom's bed. I did not know what happened but I had a big ass knot on my head. My mom told me that I fell out of the bed. I did not go to school for almost a week. We ended up moving out of that house and back in with my grandma for a little while until we went back to a shelter.

I thought stuff like this only happened on TV

When we got back in school, kids fucked with me every day. So, one day I told Brah that these boys were bothering me in class. Later that night we made plans to fuck one of them up, on site. When we got to school that morning we caught up with them in the auditorium. There were three of them, and Brah approached them and asked, "Why do y'all keep fucking with my brother". The smallest one out the group stepped up to Brah and sprayed him in the face with his asthma pump "puff". Brah picked him up and slammed him on his head "DOOM". His clicked spread like the sea and got out of there. They were looking like (and saying) "Damn, let me get out the way for big homie, he earth quaking motha fuckas". The teacher did not catch us at that time. Brah and I separated-- I went to class and got into a fight with another one of the boys. He was standing there shaking his dick at me, from between the classroom partitions. So we got into a scuffle. The principal came down to the classroom, grabbed me by the back of my shirt, and skipped me down the hall and stairs, I jerked away from him and he fell down the stairs. The school called my mom, at work and she had to come and get me. She walked all the way from her job. She came with a yellow plastic baseball bat and whipped my ass all the way to the shelter. I wanted her to listen to me and I tried to tell her that people always messed with, but she would not listen. She was just hitting me with a bat. Therefore, I haled off and slapped her ass. She told me "mother fucker you crazy, you gon' put yo' hands on me" "I got something for that ass" The rest of that night was quiet. The next morning, she told us "get up and get dressed"

She sent my brothers off to school. And she said to me

"Pig, We got somewhere to go"

We walked to the bus stop and waited. My mom did not really say much. We took a long ride. We approached a big building. I remember this vividly. We got to an office and they gave us two lunch vouchers to go down to the cafeteria and get something to eat. When we got finished eating, we went back to the office, and my mom started talking to this man. She turned to me and asked me if I liked it there and I told her I did. I only said that because I liked the cafeteria and I was happy to have something to eat. Then she told me I was staying here for a while, so these people could help me. I still did not know where I was, until I saw these two big country white motha fucka standing behind me. I saw how they were dressed and it all hit me. I was at the nut house! She had taken me to *Hart Grove Hospital*. I tried to tell my mom; I did not want to stay there. She told me "you have to so these people can help you and find out what's wrong with you". The men grabbed me and took me upstairs and I snapped; I was kicking and screaming. They put me in this room with padded walls and a steel table. I remember watching this guy bring in these thick leather straps and he strapped me to the table. They left the room and came back a little while later to check on me to see if I calmed down. (Which I did) They unstrapped me and showed me my room; it had like four or five beds in it. There were cameras in the corner of the rooms and the doors had Sargent locks on them. This guy came and got me and took me to the office. We sat down and talked about many things. He told me if I was good I would pass a level every week; it's

12 levels of the program. If I had acted out, I would have to go back a level. My first week was good, so I passed the 1st level. They allowed me to call home. I called my mom and she was still living in the shelter. I was sitting there on the phone talking to her and telling her I wanted to come home; I was crying and begging her

"please come get me".

I saw that there was a little boy sitting next to me while I was talking to my mom. The next thing I know, I heard the dial tone. He pushed the receiver and ended my call! I turned to him and asked him

"why did you just do that?!"

his response was

"I didn't do it, he did it".

I asked him

"who did it?"

and he said, again

"He did it, I didn't do it".

Then I said to him

"we are the only two here, who did it?"

I got tired and snapped and I just beat his ass with the phone. Whoever the "he" was should have helped him get me up off his ass. It took about three people to get me off him. They took me back to the padded room but they did not strap me down this time. They wanted me to calm down but, I was so mad. I was beating on the window and cracked it so they came back and strapped me down. I still did not calm down and they came back and shot me up with a big ass needle. I woke up in my room (I thought stuff like this only happened on TV) with this man in my room. He came to talk to me and told me, I had to go down a level. He gave me some money and let me use the phone. I wanted to go home so bad. I kept it cool and started passing levels. The rewards got better with every level. The second level I received game room privileges. The third level, I was able to stay up late and pick a movie to watch. The fourth level, I was allowed to go swimming. Around the 8th week, my mom came to visit, in the 9th week I was able to go down to the cafeteria, and in the 12th week, I finally went home. I was so happy that day.

Sex for Payment

We moved out of the shelter and back into my grandma's house. As usual, my mom couldn't live under my grandmas roof for long. She went back to selling crack so she could get us a place to stay. My mom got her money together and we moved into a building on the corner of Pine. It was called *Pine Building*. I liked that we finally had a place of our own. So, back To school we went. This was our second to third time transferring to How School that year. There was this one girl in school named Shanell, she use to always mess with me. My teachers use to tell me, she'd only mess with me because she liked me. She would always deny it. One day in school; I was throwing spitballs on the ceiling. One fell on Shanell's desk. We got into an argument. She got up and hit me in the face with a chair about four or five times! She dropped the chair and took off running. I ran behind her and saw Brah. I told him

"this bitch just hit me with a chair"

he told me "you better beat that bitches ass"

I chased her to the principal's office; she ran behind the counter and told me

"you can't come back here"

I went back there and beat her ass. We tore the office up! I think I broke two computers. The police came and took me home. As we pulled up in the police car, my little brother was walking up to the house. He had ditched school. He was walking with his friend Pooh and they had a dog with them. My mom was sitting there talking to her friend and she said, "Look at this shit! This mother fucker pulled up in a police car. And this mother fucker walking up like he been in school all day"

"both of you mother fuckers can get upstairs. I am whooping y'all ass" "Pooh you can take yo ass home, I am telling yo mama. If she doesn't already know"

That dog was looking confused like a mother fucker. He was looking like

"I was a free puppy until these two mother fuckers caught me. Where are y'all taking me, to another dogfight? I just got out of one of those!"

I swear that dog looked at my mom like

"ma'am, tell them to let me go!"

She said just that "where the hell did you get the dog from? Let that mother fucking dog go"

that dog took off running. When we got upstairs, I asked my little brother

"what did you do?"

He said, "I ditched school. What did you do?"

I said, "I beat Shanell ass for hitting me with a chair"

My mom walked in with a jump rope and said "who's first?"

    A lot of crazy shit happened in that *Pine Building*. One of the memories that stood out was this one time: my mom had this bike; she rode around on it almost every day. She let a woman ride it one day and the woman came back without it. I remember it like it was yesterday, she went to a store and she left the bike outside. She came back and told my mom somebody stole it and my mom put her out and told the woman not to come back without it. The woman did not come back for a couple of days. My uncle

Mud found the woman and brought her back to my mom. My mom asked her if she found the bike and the woman said

"no"

Then my mom asked her how she was going to pay her for the bike. My mom told her

"well I guess you're going to be fucking people until you make my money"

My mom told my uncle to go and

"fuck that bitch"

and all of my uncles came over. My mom sat in her window and asked every guy that walked up

"Do you want some pussy?"

She even asked us if we wanted our dicks sucked. We all said no. Brah told her

"mom, you know you wrong for doing that"

I remember opening up a door and seeing one uncle fucking her, then opening another door and another uncle fucking her. (I saw a lot of ass, titties, and pussy in my younger days) The first chance the lady got she climbed out of the window and she ran to the police station. About an hour later, the police came and picked my mom and uncle mud up! They let them go because my mom told the police the lady was willing to pay off the bike she stole by having sex.

Double Jugging

When we lived in the Pine Building, my mom use to sell a lot of drugs; she would have a lot of Jabs just sitting around on the table. One day, Brah and I took one. My cousin, uncle, and a couple of her friends were there. They were all in the kitchen-smoking crack. We did not think she would notice one of the Jabs was missing; because we had done it before. We were wrong. My mom walked in the room and said,

"where the fuck is my shit"

Everyone responded "I didn't take that shit"

She made everybody strip—ass naked! My brothers and I sat back and watched. My mom stuck her fingers in my cousin and the other female's pussy. She made my Uncle Tony put his hand on the table then asked him

"where is my shit"

He replied "I didn't take anything"

"Crack" She whacked his hand with the hammer.

She said

"where's my shit, Tony?"

"Crack"

"somebody has my shit and somebody is going to give it to me"

She broke his hand with that hammer. I started to feel bad since we were the ones that took it. That next day I saw my Uncle. He gave me a look as if he knew we had taken her shit. My mom was so into her drug life. She wanted more for us and herself; she started doubling jugging. She was getting Jabs from Doe Boy and buying from somebody else. She was selling both on Doe Boy's block. Word got back to Doe Boy and he started looking for my mom. One day my little brother and I were sitting in the house. We heard

"Boom, Boom"

Tip(Doe Boy's guy- one of the Moe's) kicked in the back door, Tango (Moe) kicked in the front door, and Doe Boys' fat ass came thru our window. My mom was not home at the time. They left, but before they did, they threw cocktail bombs on the back porch, and burnt it up. When my mom heard Doe Boy was looking for her; she started coming in thru the back door. One day she was coming in and two fat Mexican chicks were waiting for her in the back of the house. Doe Boy did not really know my mom at the time; he did not know she had hands. She ended up beating both of those bitches asses. When Doe Boy heard about it he was pissed. Later on that day, Doe Boy caught my mom and hit her in the eye. Brah found out that Doe Boy hit her in the eye. He told everybody that he was going to kill him. The brothers came and talked to Brah and told him he cannot be just going around saying he was going to kill one of the brothers (Moe's). Brah said

"but this nigga hit my mom in the eye".

They told him that they were going to talk to Doe Boy; that shit never happen, so I guess Brah just left that shit alone. I guess time heals everything because Brah and Doe Boy eventually got back cool.

Karma

One day Brah, my cousin, one of the guys, and I-- we all had this idea of robbing a weed spot. We had two guns; one of them was broken and the other one did not have a clip. Well, the plan was for my brother and me to go in and rob them. But when we got up to the spot, I chicken out, so I passed the gun to my cousin. I was about ten years old at the time. I guess this was my initiation to hang around the big guys. When we got into the hallway of the weed spot, there was a girl-serving weed. My cousin asked her for a couple of nickel bags. As she pulled the weed out; my cousin pulled his gun on her, then my brother pulled his gun out. The girl broke down in tears, and said,

"I'm sorry, I'm sorry, please don't kill me. Take it, take it all".

My cousin told her

"shut the fuck up"

he grabbed her by her hair, and we took her up the stairs. She took us into an apartment, we walked into the living room, and there was a table full of weed. We grabbed the weed; ran out the apartment, down the stairs, around the corner, and through an alley. That is when I had to make a pit stop. I ran out of breath, I was a fat kid and I could not run any longer. I stopped in this garage doorway. I then heard these guys and saw this red beam come up the alley. I knew my fat ass was about to be bacon. They saw me and told me to come here. As I was walking towards them, Brah came back for me pointing his gun at them; he said,

"get the fuck away from my brother".

They took off running, and we got away. *God has plans for me.* We split the weed up and went to my pops house; as if nothing happened.

A couple months later, my brother and I were at my grandmother's house. My grandmother kicked us out that night, she said to us,

"get out my house, and go find y'all mama".

It was like two or three o'clock in the morning (like clockwork. This was the time she was good and drunk. She would just be sitting there thinking about my mom leaving her kids. She would come up and hit us with those stale ass punches. She would tell us "y'all are always playing with my wigs, I am going to catch you while you're sleeping" and that's what she did); it was snowing at the time. Brah was working at this Blow spot. He had just bought a car, it was a Pontiac diplomat, and the driver's side was smashed in, so we had to get in on the passenger side. My mom lived all the way on the other side of town, with one of her boyfriends. When we got in the car, I was going to driving, but as I was about to pull off the car would not move. Brah checked to find out what was wrong, and the tire was flat. We walked back over to my grandmother's house, knocked on her door, and she said

"Didn't I tell y'all to go find y'all mama".

Brah and I went back to the car and fell asleep. A little while later; I woke up to a tapping sound on the passenger side window

"tap, tap".

I was in the driver's seat. I opened my eyes and there was a guy tapping on the window with a gun! I closed my eyes and thought to myself "fuck this, I'm gon let my brother wake up to these problems"

so I continued to play as if I was asleep. He tapped again; that is when Brah woke up.

The guy with the gun told my brother,

"open up this motha fucking do' ".

Brah opened the door; he asked Brah

"where the shit at"

Brah said, "what shit? I don't have nothin,"

he said "you little motha fuckas been out here hustlin' all night y'all got something"

I was still playing like I was asleep, he reached over to me and poked me with the gun,

then said "little motha fucka wake up, what you got".

I said, "I don't have anything".

Since we were sleeping in the car; to stay warm, I had on three coats. One of them was a red and black Fubu coat. I had just bought it. He told me to take the coats off and give them to him. He then told Brah to step out of the car and come with him. Brah told him

"I'm not going nowhere with you"

he pointed the gun at me and told Brah

"I'm gon shoot him"

That's when my brother told him

"Okay I'll take you to the shit"

He took my brother to the alley. I got out the car, ran back over to my grandmother house, and banged on her door. My uncle Wayne came to the door and I told him

"some guy took my brother in the alley with a gun to his head. He tried to rob us."

Then I heard a gunshot! I started to cry. I just knew they killed my brother. A few minutes later, I saw my brother run from across the street, past Mr. Jones funeral home, it was a car following him! My brother got a couple of houses away from our grandma's house. That same guy got out of the car; grabbed my brother by the back of his neck, and put the gun to his head. My brother yelled out

"he's getting the shit for you right now".

The guy told my brother

"stop lying, that's yo grandma's house little mother fucker"

Then hit my brother in his face two times with the gun. My brother ran on to my grandma's porch he was pouring blood from his mouth and his nose .WELL my grandma let us back in that night, we laid down on the couch and went to sleep. She did not kick us out again after that incident. Karma is a bitch!

***

    One day I went to school and kids were talking about me because I had on dirty clothes from the previous day. I told the teacher and her way of making things better was putting me in front of the classroom in a desk next to hers Well, the kids just wouldn't leave me alone. I felt like she made a bad choice putting me on Front Street. While she was writing on the blackboard; kids were still picking with me, and throwing things at me. I turned around and looked at them. She turned to me and told me to turn around and do my work. So, I kicked the desk at her and it tipped over and broke her leg! She went "SIDEWAYS" (in my Kevin Gates voice) She fell and her head bounced off the side of the desk. I jumped over her and said, "That's what you get you dumb bitch...putting me in front of the class and got these kids still fucking with me".

I walked out of the classroom. She ended up pressing charges on me and had me locked up. I spent a couple of weeks in a juvenile facility and then I went to court; she came over, and talked to me. I told her

"I am sorry that I broke your leg". "I was just mad that you put me in front of the class, because that did not help the situation. It actually made everything worse".

She said, "You're not sorry because you jumped up and cursed me out".

I told her "I am sorry. I was just mad".

We went in front of the judge and she had the charges dropped. I asked the judge if I could live with my grandma, because I was tired of going in and out of shelters with my mom. The judge turned to my grandma and asked her if this was alright. My grandma was looking like

"where the fuck did this come from. I was just taking your little fat ass to court. You gon put me on front street in front of them judge" She had no choice but to say yes.

Back to Grandma's

One morning, I woke up and it was this guy standing over me. I got up, went in my grandma's room, and asked her
"who is this guy in our house?"
She grabbed me, looked me directly in my eyes, and whispered to me
"it's your uncle Snuffy he just got out of jail from doing 16 years…you need to stay away from him".
So, one day we were sitting on the front porch and we saw the police jump out on Snuffy. The began searching him. One of the police pulled a gun and put it to the back of Snuffy's head. He told the officer
"look man gets your gun off of my head".
After repeatedly asking the officer to take the gun off his head, the officer finally listened to the request and put the gun back in the holster. Uncle Snuffy turned around and knocked his ass out! I've never seen anything like it; he flew through the air (it looked like something out of a comedy movie) and his partner took off running!! I was looking like
"you ain't gone help your partner?"
My uncle turned around and I thought he was going to take off running, but he did not. He turned around; started looking for something, and picked up a mail tray (a U.S. postal flat hard plastic mail tray. I have no idea what it was doing sitting there. This is Chicago, it's no telling) and beat the officer repeatedly in the face with it!!! I think the

police department locked down because our whole block was filled with police cars. He got out of jail that next day. He was beaten badly, but he survived. I looked at him differently after that.

When I moved in with my grandma, I would sit around her a lot. She liked to play the lottery. One time I put her lottery ticket in her bible for good luck. When I showed her where I put it, she said,

"don't play with god like that"

and she slapped the shit out of me. The next day she came to me and secretly hand-shaked (that is a technical term) me $40 and told me she won the lottery. I went straight to the discount mall! I bought a phony pleather coat, a new shirt, and some jeans. It was hot that day but I wanted to show my shit off

"I don't stink today. No ketchup stains or nothing"

I liked money and I wanted to have my own. My mama was a hustler so I was born a hustler. I started on the block working security for the guys. Working security, you would have to sit on the corner and yell out "mama" if you saw the police and you would get $5 whenever the guy you're looking out for was done with their pack. Their pack would be 25 rocks of cocaine. Every rock was worth $5; you make $25 and you turn in $100 and you pay your look out $5. I remember one time my uncle Snuffy got a Jab and he wanted me to work security for him, but I had something to do. When uncle Snuffy was done with his Jab; Tip came to pick up, he gave Tip $25 and kept $100 and told Tip

"that's how it goes".

Tip told him "it's the other way around".

He told Tip "You must be crazy" "You think I am going to be looking this way and that way for the police and I am selling this shit to people I don't even know. You better get out my basement fat boy".

So Tip ran to Doe Boy and Doe Boy came down to talk to him. Uncle Snuffy told him "I am going to tell you like I told the other fat boy--get the fuck out my face". He ripped off his shirt and was pounding his chest yelling

"you see my motha fucking Bench Marks, nigga, I ain't no motha fucking joke; I don't have shit for you".

Doe Boy moved around.

Do Not Disturb

There were times when my uncle Larry would stay up all night working Jabs for Tango and Tip. It would eventually come to the point where he would get tired. He would stay in his room and smoke crack until he fell asleep. He was like a fucking bear. He would go smoke some crack and hibernate. Well this was one of those times: He told Tip and Tango that he fucked the Jab up and smoked it. They whooped his ass. He locked himself in his room, wrote a sign on the door "Do not disturb" My uncle Snuffy knocked on the door anyways, and asked him for a lighter. Larry opened the door and said,

"DO NOT DISTURB"

and he slammed the door. Snuffy knocked on the door again. He said,

"I know you have a lighter"

Larry opened the door and pointed to the sign

"Read the sign—DO.NOT.DISTURB",

and tried to slam the door again. Uncle Snuffy kicked the door in. He went in the room and beat the fuck out of Larry. Snuffy lifted Larry over his head and body slammed him into the closet (My uncle Jerry was a hoarder and dumpster diver. He had TV's, Old microwaves and VCR's in his closet) Snuffy jumped in the closet on Larry like a wild ape! (Picture Caesar attacking Koba in the *Dawn of the Planet of the Apes)* I wish I had a camera to capture that footage I would've yelled out "Worldstar!!!"

Shit Happens

The next morning, I was walking thru the living room and I heard my uncle Snuffy yelled out

"somebody bring me some tissueeeee".

I yelled out

"you should've thought about that before you sat your ass down".

He said, "Go get me some tissue you fat ass boy"

I told him "hell nawl"

He said while laughing "okay it's a towel in here"

I yelled out "you better not wipe your ass with my towel"

The next thing you know, he walked out of the bathroom. My towel was soaking in the sink—with shit on it. I asked him

"why did you wipe your ass with my towel, you nasty mother fucker"

I ran and told my grandma. She said,

"I thought I told you to stay away from that crazy ass boy. Come here and get you another towel. And stay the hell away from him"

Am I my Brother's Keeper? Yes I am

What happened to Hood grandmas?

The definition of a hood grandma-

They were there for all of their grandkids and neighborhood kids, because the drug epidemic ruined their own children's lives. We had four hood grandmas in the neighborhood; My grandma- Ms. Jackson, Ms. Matthews, Ms. Ward, and Ms. Kelly (rumor has it that my grandma shot at Ms. Kelly). A lot of the time if we were hungry and didn't have a place to stay. The neighborhood kids had these four grandmas to choose from. My grandma and Ms. Matthews had the same style of basements. They had them set up like barn stalls with sheets as dividers for room (but, it also gave their nothing ass kids a place to toke up). So, it was nothing to pull back a sheet and see our parents smoking crack. We use to always walk past the "rooms" and hear loud sizzles "ttttsssssss" "pop"

We had a couple of hood grandmas, whom families were affected by the drug epidemic. One in particular was Ms. Ward. This was my cousin, by marriages, house. Their basement wasn't set up like barn yards. They had actual bedrooms. People in their family were hustlers and had real jobs. Except one guy; Tyrone, he was dating my mom. Their family was real uppity. They looked down on all of the families that had crack heads in them.

One day, I was playing at Ms. Matthew house. She had a granddaughter named Shannon. I got into with her and her little sister. They both attacked me like two wild cats. A couple of hours later, I caught Shannon on the side of her grandma's house and I busted her head with a brick. Brah had a crush on Shannon. But she was my friend Eric's girlfriend. Later that day, I was walking out of the corner store and Brah came out of nowhere and grabbed me. He yelled out

"Ms. Matthews I caught him for you"

I said "Brah no! Please let me go, let me go"

Ms. Mathews (Shannon's crazy ass grandma) was walking towards me with Shannon. She said,

"Little mother fucker you busted my grand baby head"

As soon as Brah let me go, Ms. Matthews grabbed me by the back of my shirt and whooped me with an extension cord. I somehow managed to get free and ran down to my grandma's house. I told my grandma

"Ms. Matthews just beat me with a cord"

While I was telling her the story, she looked my back and saw I had welts all over my body. Then, Ms. Matthews began knocking on our front door

"Tell that little bastard to get his ass back out here"

My grandma opened up the door and snapped!

"Why the fuck did you beat my grandson with a fucking extension cord. Now he has welts all over his body. I should call the police on your ass"

Grandma was ready to box! Ms. Matthews said,

"He busted my grand baby head, she had to go to the hospital and get stiches"

Then it all turned around on me and my grandma was ready to whoop my ass. My grandma told me that she was going to call my dad over to handle me; that never happened. A few days later, my brothers and I were getting out of school and Brah saw Shannon and walked up to her and put his arms around her. They walked off talking, that is when Eric saw them. Eric walked up to Brah and asked,

"Why do you have your arms around my girl"

Brah said,

"This ain't your girl"

They got into an argument. Brah was a little older than Eric was. Eric told him

"I am going to get Octavia to fuck you up"

Octavia was Eric's man-beater-beast of a cousin. I went off to work. By the way, I worked in the Chicago discount mall, selling bootlegs music and cassette tapes/ restaurant. Brah went home. A few hours later when I got off work, I was excited to watch the new movie *The Player's Club* that had just came out. I sat down to put the tape into the VCR and I heard the ice cream truck coming up the street. I gave my brothers some money to bring back some ice cream, and we would all watch the movie together. A little while later, my little cousin came running in the house and told me,

"Yo brothers are outside getting into with Octavia".

(Okay, this is from what I heard how the fight started) Eric went and told Octavia that Brah was supposed to be whopping her ass (he had to lie to Octavia that Brah was talking about her—she was not just going to just jump into them fighting over a girl) Brah and Donnell were at the ice-cream truck and Octavia approached them and said

"Huggie you got a problem with me? You are going around telling people you gon' whoop my ass?"

Brah said "man I don't know what the fuck you are talking about"

My little brother jumped in front of Brah and said "man you better get out my brothers face"

She said "move little boy" "so Hug, I just asked you a question"

Donnell repeated himself "you better get out my brothers face!"

Next thing you know; she hit him in the nose "I told yo' little ass"

Brah dropped the ice cream's and punched Octavia. She turned her head like "what the fuck. It's on now"

By this point, I was on my way to them. All I saw was Brah getting socked up by Octavia; he couldn't do anything with that big bitch. I was trying to get to them but the gate was locked. I was trying to unlock it and Brah was trying to get in the gate. He was trying to get away from that bitch. Brah turned around as he was trying to get in the gate. Octavia picked up a brick and busted Brah in the face with it. I looked at Eric and pointed,

"Eric I am fucking you up, dude"

And I did too. I whooped his ass. The Moe's came and picked Brah up and were about to violate him for getting into with a sister. But, they didn't because Brah explained to them what happened. They joked with him

"Man, you went up against Octavia without a bat, a stick, or something?"

Brah, Tip, Tango and I had just left the corner store; we were walking towards my grandma's house. As we got closer, we heard yelling, my uncle Snuffy was arguing with my grandma. He told her

"you ain't grown, you ain't grown, you can't curse at me".

She told him

"I am your fucking mama" "I want your crazy ass out my house".

Brah jumped in uncle Snuffy's face and told him,

"You better stop talking to my grandma like that".

Snuffy said, "You better stay out of grown folks business and stay in a child's place".

Brah said, "You ain't going to be talking to my grandma like that".

Uncle Snuffy got that crazy fucked up look in his eyes, "look fat ass boy take you and your punk ass friends and get the fuck on".

Brah must have said something else and uncle Snuffy snapped and knocked Brah the fuck out. He hit Brah with an upper cut; Brah did a backflip over my grandma's bed and landed in the corner! I looked over at Tip and Tango like

"are y'all gon' help?"

They said, "Fuck this shit. This is family business"

And walked out.

In the next few days, there was a big setback in my life. Brah and I shared a room. We both use to hustle together. Brah was the Jab man for the night shift. He passed out Jabs. He had a G pack; (12 jabs) He kept $200 and turned in $1000. One day Brah and I were up all night passing out Jabs. We ran threw two G packs. I sat in the room and had the Jabs ready for Brah. He would go back to the block and sell them. I had to stay in the room and watch our shit because all of our uncles were crack heads. He was running back and forth thru the house; creating a lot of traffic. I got this Mickey Mouse cup and tied a long string around it. I told him to stop running in and out of the house; I had a plan, so he did not have to keep running past my grandma's door. I told him

"yell up to the window when you need a Jab. I will lower it to you in this Mickey Mouse cup"

We did that all night. Brah got finished with the fourth G pack; somehow, I had fallen asleep. I woke up to Brah running up the stairs and beating on the door

"Let me in! Let me in"

I got up and I heard my grandma say

"get his ass out of my house. I am tired of his ass running in and out of this house selling drugs"

I let Brah in the room. He pulled a G pack out of his coat and asked me

"Brah, where should I put it"

I told him

"let's put it in the closet"

But, we would have had to move our entertainment stand; it was blocking the closet door. By the time we were about to move it; the police were at our bedroom door trying to kick it down. One of the officers said

"Huggie, open the door!"

The next thing you know Brah panicked, and threw the G pack out of the window. I heard an officer yell

"thanks"

Brah threw it right into a police officer's hands. Brah turned to me and said

"Brah, take this case for me"

I did not even have to think about it; I would do anything for my brother. I said

"okay"

Brah opened the door for them. I recognized one of the officers; we all called him

"Urkle". As they came in, I said,

"it belongs to me"

He said,

"That's not yours. It's Huggie's"

They searched the room and did not find anything else but money. They put the cuffs on Brah. I gave him a hug and they took him. I cried all that night.

       That next morning Tip came to the house and asked me where my brother was. I told him

"he got locked up last night" "the police were after him and my grandma let them in on him and he got caught with the whole G pack".

Tip asked, "so where is the money"

I told him, "the police took it all" I then told him "I tried to take the case but they wouldn't let me"

Tip said "they wouldn't let you take the case because you would've gotten right out"

"but your brother, he's a goner" He walked off.

I was glad he did walk off, because I had six hundred dollars in my pocket. As it turned out the police did not take the money. Then I went to school. I asked these two girls; Shanell and Rene to go to the movies with me. I told them

"it's on me"

I was on a punishment at the time; but I was taking them anyways.

When I got home from school, I saw my bedroom door kicked off the hinges! I went downstairs and told my grandma that somebody kicked my door in. I walked outside and I saw my uncle Snuffy walking up the street holding all of my clothes! I asked him

"what the fuck are you doing with all of my clothes"

He said, "move! Get the FUCK out my face fat boy!"

The next thing you know, while we were talking, Tango came up behind him and hit him in the back of the head with a baseball bat.

"Bing"

His eyes rolled to the back of his head. He fell straight backwards and his head bounced off the ground. Brah's other guy; Maine jumped on him and broke a beer bottle across his face. My uncle Jerry stood there watching. I picked up my clothes. And I walked back to the house. My grandma sat on the porch yelling

"get off of him"

While on the phone with the police.

"get off him"

After the ambulance came and picked my uncle up, my uncle Jerry came in the house. I asked him

"why didn't you help your brother?"

"Doe Boy had a gun" "don't jump in it" He replied

I went into the house and got dressed and went to the movies. When I got back home; I got my ass whooped. I did not care. I had a good time; I took two girls to the movies and old country buffet.

2

"That created the hunger and that makes a monster. Got the game from our mama, that's some ill shit"

        -Yo Gotti

"I keep telling you to stay away from that crazy ass boy"

        -Margret Jackson

My First Jab

I was 12 years olds. My mama and Brah were in jail, so I had to get out there so I could take care of my little brother. I started on the corner, working security. I would yell "mama"

when I saw the police. I remember it like it was yesterday; my auntie Lynn gave me my first jab. I was happy to work on the block. Well, I was happy and nervous at the same time. When I got out to the block, so many clucks surrounded me; I dropped all 25 of my rocks. I yelled loud and aggressively

"stop and nobody move"

I picked up all of my rocks. I sold all 25 of them in less than one minute! I said to myself

"this shit is bidnezzzz"

Doe Boy found out I was working on the block. He talked to me and told me

"you are too young to be working the block. But, you can work security"

I went back to security, but on the night shift when he was not around; I went back to working Jabs. Later on that day, I got into with my uncle Snuffy, again. We were talking and I called him a "bitch" He punched me in the chest and knocked the wind out of me. I got up and tried to play it off. He knew I called him a bitch, but I tried to tell him that I called him a snitch. I went and told my grandma and she said,

"I keep telling you to stay away from that crazy ass boy"

My move with my Auntie

Later on that week, my mama got out of jail on house arrest. She was only out for a couple of days and she got into with my grandma (her mom). My grandma cut the cord (phone line) on her house arrest box! My mama had just got a 50 jab. She took the 50 off it and told me

"get it off"

So, I was working for no pay but it was all good. It only took a couple hours for the police to get there and hauled her off to the county. My grandma told them

"get her ass out of my house. I am tired of her selling drugs out of my house and not giving me any money!"

She went back to jail.

My grandma got sick; she had one of her legs amputated, and they tried to cut off the other leg, but she would not let them. She said it was her time to go, and my brother and I had to move in with my auntie. My grandma moved in with my auntie Bertha. Well, with my mama locked up…they gave her like 8 years in prison (she only had to do four). We went to stay with my auntie Bobbi. My little brother and I were still going to How school at the time. We were still getting in trouble at How. I got in to it with Shanell again; the girl that hit me in my face with a chair. Well, she hit me again; she hit me in my face and ran into the girl's bathroom. She ran into one of the bathroom stalls and locked the door. I threw a metal garbage can over the stall and it hit her in the face. She came out of the stall bleeding everywhere! By this time, How school was tired of me and my brothers. They kick me out. I do not think my aunt wanted us to go to that school anyways. She had to wake us up and take us to school every day and all we were doing was getting into trouble. My aunt enrolled us into Pablo. We didn't have too much of an education (from all the school we missed jumping from shelter to shelter) and it was hard for us to catch up with other students at Pablo. I had a hard time with reading and math. There was this teacher, Mrs. Zadab. She took me and a couple other students with her. She helped me a lot and when she was teaching me, I caught on so much faster than the other students. Sometimes she would have me help other students. One day, I got into with this girl named Nicole. I guess her brothers had this gang thing going on called "the Ruff Ryder's" I got into it with her in the classroom where Mrs. Zadab taught us. Nicole would not stop talking about what her brothers were going to do to me after school. I told her

"look, they ain't gonna do shit to me" I said "fuck the Ruff Ryder's".

Later that day after school, I told my cousin Raymond what happened, as I was walking home. Nicole left school early so as we got closer to the house we saw this big crowd of dudes. All I saw was Nicole pointing her finger at me. It was like 10 to 20 guys approaching me and they asked me why I put my hands on their sister?

I told them "your sister is lying, I didn't touch her… all we did is argue". They started jumping on me. One of the guys pulled out a gun and hit me in head with it. I couldn't see anything because my head was bleeding. So, I took off and ran. When we got to the house my big cousin's; Poncho and Reggie asked me what happened and I told them "I just got jumped" and they asked my cousin Raymond "why the fuck don't you have any marks or knots on you if you were fighting together"

After all of that shit; my cousins and I walked around the corner to Nicole's house. When we got there, they wanted me to fight Nicole's brother. But, my head was too swollen and I was feeling dizzy, so we all went back to the house and life went on. That winter my grandma died; I was so sad. I am thankful that she was always there for me.

Graduating in the upstairs neighbors Air Force One's

When we lived in my aunt's house, I always felt left out. I remember my 8th grade graduation; I did not have anything to wear. I asked my aunt to buy me a pair of dress shoes,

she said

"no" "go look upstairs in one of my empty apartments"

(my aunt had rental property. She also was getting a check for being my guardian while my mother was locked up). I found a beat up pair of air forces. I sat upstairs, and talked to my big cousin Marquita. I told her that I didn't have anything to wear to my graduation and how I didn't want to go. She told me that I only get one--8th grade graduation so I might as well go. I just wanted a pair of dress shoes; it didn't matter what clothes I had to wear because I had a cap and gown over them anyways. But, I ended up going. I walked across the stage. My family didn't even end up making it to my graduation. My cousin Raymond had to go to summer school before he could graduate.

Well that summer, I got into my first fight of the summer, with a guy named Mookey. He just kept fucking with me. My cousin and everyone on the block kept telling me how scared I was of Mookey and that I did not want to fight him. It was not that I was scared; I just did not like to fight. One day I said to myself "fuck it" and in order for him to stop fucking with me, I was just going to get out here and whoop his ass. So, I did it and he left me alone for a while. My second fight that summer was with this guy who tried to take my little brothers baseball bat. I caught him in the act and we started fighting. I was getting the best of him so he took off running. A couple days later, we were all playing hide and go seek, in both of the Central park alley's, on the block. I found my little brother at the end of one alley. The next thing you know, 10 guys start chasing us. They caught my little brother, so I had to go back; I couldn't leave him. There was a grown man there and he told me to fight one on one with the kid who tried to take the bat from my little brother, a couple days ago. As soon as we started fighting and they saw I was getting the best of him; they all started jumping me. I looked up and saw that my brother took off running! I ended up in the backyard of a girl I went to Pablo with. She yelled,

"that's Raymond's cousin y'all are jumping on!"

I yelled back to her "go and get my cousin!"

Ten kids and a grown man jumped me, and I came out of it with only a busted lip. I ran back down to the house and I got up with my cousins. As we were running back up the street, we ran into my cousin LaFea, who was just getting off work. We all ran back to the house to get his gun. We went over to the block looking for them and they were nowhere to be found and we went back home. I tried to sit in the basement because my face was all fucked up but my auntie called us up for dinner. My cousin was trying to tell me

"just stay downstairs".

I had been outside playing all day so I was hungry and hadn't eaten anything. I went upstairs to eat, my auntie brought my plate of food; she asked me "boy, what happened to your damn face?"

I told her "nothing" she said "your ass had been out there fighting again"

and she left it at. I thought I was going to get in trouble. As I previously mention, my cousin was going to summer school that year and the boys that jumped me were also attending summer school. Well, one of the guys that jumped me was in the bathroom bragging about what he had done. To his surprise, my cousin was also in there. My cousin Raymond let him finish his story. Raymond hit him in his shit and bounced his head off the toilet. My cousin came home and told me what happened and he told us to be up there everyday after school. Every day, my little brother and I walked up to the school with a bat and a hammer. One day, we walked up to the school and the guy that I had got into it with and his guys were up there waiting for him. They didn't recognize me. My little brother and I sat on a school playground bench and waited on my cousin. As soon as my cuz walked out the door, they approached him and tried to jump on him. My brother and I rushed over to him. They thought he was there by himself. We didn't fight that day; it just was a bunch of arguing. They didn't want to run up because my little brother and I had a bat and hammer. We all walked home; but we kept going up there, day after day. Then one day, my brother and I were walking out of the front door; my auntie stopped us, and told us

"y'all aren't going anywhere".

I tried to come up with every excuse in the book so we could leave and go up to the school with my cousin. My cousin walked in the door 20 minutes later. He was all beat up and asked us "why the hell didn't y'all come up to the school?"

I told him "yo mom wouldn't let us leave"

He said "them motherfuckers jumped on me! I didn't have to fight until yo ass moved here".

He was mad at us for a while. But, what could we have done? He eventually got over it. A while later, he graduated. This is when I really starting feeling left out, while living with my auntie. When it was time for RAYMOND to graduate; they went and bought him dress shoes and dress clothes! I was looking at him and her like

"man, I couldn't even get a pair of dress shoes from payless, that's all I was really asking for". My auntie saw how I was looking. She told me

"I will get you something later"

She asked me what I wanted. I told her

"a jean outfit"

I never got the outfit; she never mentioned it and neither did I. I was just thankful that she let us live with her. We could have been living in the street.

My Mama Came Home

Later on that summer, I got to see Brah for the first time in like two years. The first thing he said to me was

"damn boy y'all getting skinny as hell. I already know auntie Bobbi doesn't play about that fridge".

I was happy to see my brother. After he got out of the "little Joliet" (Juvie) he was living in a group home, he didn't have a place to go. My auntie did not want him at her house and my dad did not want him at his house either. He had to stay at a group home, until to my mom got out of jail. Now the summer vacation was over; it was time for me to go to high school. I went to high school with; Tyra, Shakira, and Calvina. They all use to knock on my window and get me up for school in the morning so we could all walk together. I remember, one morning they came and got me up: we heard a gunshot on our way to school. As we all walked down the street, we met up with Nicole. As and we got farther down Augusta St. we saw this guy laying across the street by the stop sign. His brains were in his hoodie! We did not stay too long to see who it was; we had to get to school. I remember, that same day I got into my first fight, at school. This big ass fat boy would not let me cut in the lunch line; I was trying to talk to this girl. I went ahead and cut him in the line. This fat ass boy grabbed me and told me

"you better get back to where you was".

He was on some hating shit. I told him

"do not grab me no more".

He grabbed me again telling me

"get back to the end of the line".

I punched him in the nose

"splat"

blood splattered everywhere. He bent over holding his nose then I hit him in his eye

"bam"

I upper cut him in his eye! He lifted up and his eye was bleeding. He went back down and he tried to turn around to get away from me, and he busted his other eye on a pole

"dong"

Now, I saw that both of his eyes were swollen shut! I just went in and start fucking him up. When I came out of the cafeteria line, everybody was asking me

"what did you hit him with?"

They thought that I hit him with a lock; my clothes were so bloody that everybody on the outside of the cafeteria thought I killed him. One of the security guards who came and broke up the fight; pulled me into the hallway ,and told me

"Calm down Jackson look at him and look at you, you won".

I was suspended from school, and my auntie had to come pick me up. My suspension was over a few days later, my uncle took me back to school because the principal wanted to talk to my guardians. I tried to explain to my uncle

"it was not my fault; this guy put his hands on me first, and he was trying to bully me".

When my uncle and I got to the office to talk to the principal, the guy I fought had his uncle there too. When his uncle saw how little I was, he looked at him and said "you let this little ass boy beat you up"

The guy I got into a fight with, face was still swollen, and I think I permanently damaged his eyes.

After we talked to the principal my uncle left. I went to eat breakfast and everybody was still talking about the fight. I did not say anything else to him after the day we fought. I think that fight helped me get my first girlfriend; her name was Samantha. She had a friend come up and talk to me, to tell me that she liked me. We got up with each other and we kicked it for like a month or two. We talked on the phone, sat out in front of the school, and kissed. She was my first girl, so I did not really know what to do. I would write her poetry. We would kiss at our lockers and we would talk over the phone. My auntie never liked it when she called the house though. My aunt would always tell me

"stop having all these fast ass girls calling my phone".

We went to a homecoming party for school and I was dancing with my friend Tyra. I got embarrassed because my girlfriend caught me dancing with her. I just sat down for the rest of the night. Samantha wanted to dance with me and I would not dance with her. I think she was mad I danced with Tyra instead of her, because when we got back to school Samantha told one of her friends to come and tell me that it was over. I guess the cliché is true "you lose them the way you get them". She was sitting at a different table from me and I told her friend to tell her

"well okay, it is cool".

I went back to sit at the table I had been sitting at when I first started school with Shakira, Tyra, and Calvina. They told me from the beginning that I been acting funny since I had been with Samantha. But, that is what happens when you get into a relationship; you stop hanging around your true friends that has been with you through everything.

I was not worried about being in a relationship anyways, because my auntie told me that my mom was getting out at the end of this school year and we would be moving to Springfield. One day, the girls and I were walking home from school, and Shakira was talking about losing her virginity to her boyfriend, she said
"I want to give my virginity away to somebody that loves me, if he don't tell me he loves me before this month is over I'm done with him, who knows I might just fuck Pig".
I always had a thing for Shakira but she had a boyfriend. Ever since she said she might let me fuck I was on her ass every day on the walk home from school. We were walking home from school one day and Shakira was looking sad, I asked her what was wrong with her, and she told me she broke up with her boyfriend. I told her that everything was going to be alright, as we were about to part ways I gave her a hug, and out of nowhere, she kissed me. We had one month of school left, and almost every day that month we hung out. A week before I was about to move to Springfield. Shakira and I were standing in a crowd of our friends, and Shakira, out of the blue told me she loves me. I loved her too, she just caught me off guard with it; we were in front of a lot of our friends. I was stuck in a loss of words, all our friends started to look at me, like

"what you gonna say back".

I grabbed her by her hand and pulled her out the crowd, and said

"I love you too; I was just too shy to tell you in front of everybody".

She said, "well I'm not about to lose my virginity to somebody that don't love me, because if you love me you would've said it back in front of everybody, and you're about to move out of town".

I walked her down to her house; we sat down in her backyard and talked. I told her I did not want to leave, and I will back to see her. I tried to get her to come down to my house, but she told me

"no"

She was not ready, so I did not get to fuck. A week later, we got out of school. I mean, my auntie did not waste no time. She had my little brother and me at the train station that next day. When we got there, I started to cry, I thought about all the fun times I had staying with my auntie and cousins. I still laugh about them now to this day. Like the time my Little brother and cousin busted in on me while I was taking a shower and whooped me with belts. There was another time my cousin tricked me into coming outside and my Little brother poured a bucket of water on me from the top floor. I am so happy and grateful that my auntie and uncle took my little brother and me in. I do not know where we would be if it was not for them. I love y'all for everything y'all have done for us. Thank you Margaret Walson a.k.a Bobbi and Riley Walson (rest in peace Riley Walson).

3

"GMB, GMB, Bitch. Keep it in the family, Hug"

-Vodka

"*Life is a fight for territory.* And once you stop fighting for what you want, what you don't want will automatically take over." - *Steve Duncanson.*

"It's up to get you where you want to be and need to be" -Pig

My Move to Springfield

I moved to Springfield in the summer of 2001. My little brother and I had to move to Springfield. My mom was just getting out of jail for serving a four-year sentence in prison. My big brother was still in a group home in Joliet. When my mom got out, she came to Springfield in this program for parolees. They give you a house, job, and a ride to work every day. My little brother and I worked for this guy, whom we called "Father". I remember him being a short stocky guy with the biggest hands I have ever seen (still to this day). He gave us summer jobs. We did landscaping; planted trees, planted flowers, and cut grass. He had us working in a Grado. He had a big warehouse that my brother, my Uncle Fred and Steve, and I use to go to and unpack boxes. There were boxes of baby pampers, ripped clothes, food, laundry detergent, and other supplies. I think it was all the stuff that came from stores, which they could not sell. One day we were working in a warehouse and my little brother did not want to do any work. All he wanted to do was sleep, so he went to sleep on one of the lazy boys couches. My uncle Fred and I started the truck up and I left the passenger side door open. I went to get a big bucket of water… my little brother was laid back in the lazy boy chair. I poured a whole bucket of cold water on his face and I took off running. My little brother tried to jump on the back of the truck but my uncle peeled off and shot rocks on him. My uncle and I went a half a mile up to the Freedom gas station. My little brother chased the truck all the way to the gas station. He had to run up and down hills to catch up with us. My uncle and I got out and went in the gas station to get some snacks, as soon as I walked out of the gas station. I saw my little brother right by the end of the driveway of the gas station running full fledge. I mean buckets of sweat just pouring off him. I think the bucket of water I poured on him dried up on the run towards us. He had to have been running nonstop-- five or six blocks and it's was about 95 to 100 degrees outside. My Uncle and I weren't even in the gas station that long. I hurried up and jumped in the truck. We went back to drop the trucks off at the job site. My uncle and I left the warehouse and left my little brother there with my uncle Steve. When he got home he was not even mad anymore, we set back and laughed about it. My brother, Uncles, and I always had fun working at the warehouse. We were able to do what we wanted and it was not anybody there to watch over us. We were being paid to play most of the time and when the trucks came in with all this stuff on them, we would unload them. We would organize stuff; putting pampers in one box, food in another, and clothes in another box. Then an empty truck would come and then we would reload the empty trucks with the stuff that we organize. With Pampers, food, clothes, and detergent we would take a lot of that stuff out and take it home with us. We really did not need to pay for anything. A lot of the stuff we would sale; especially the pampers. We would work at the Bingo hall, where supplies were also delivered. We would pack the dumpster or put stuff on the side of it. After the Bingo hall closed we would come back and get the stuff, we had a nice hustle. School was about to start back and I would be starting my sophomore year; I did not want to wear any of the clothes that were coming in of the trucks. Most of the clothes had holes in them and were defective. I was talking to my mom about me being paid for the work that I was doing. She talked to father about it and let him know that I was working hard like everyone else so I expected to be paid like everyone else. Father started paying me $150 a week. I was too young to get on the payroll so he paid me cash. That was cool because school was about to start back up and it was going to be my first year going to Lanphier high school. My first year was my last year. My first day I thought "I've never seen this many white kids in my Life". I always stayed to myself; my first couples of weeks were boring until Brah moved in with us. That was one of the happiest days of my life. I finally got Brah back. The next week I went back to school and Brah went with me. Within a week of school, Brah met two guys, Jason and Trayvon.

The Team

    Brah had a thing for nicknames and everyone we met Brah gave nicknames. He called Jason "J hood" and Trayvon "little tray". Then we met up with Larry, we called him "Mike Larry" or "Laro". Then we met "Queasy" and "Resco". We met Eddie and we called him "4". Because he was a 4-corner hustler, but Brah call him "444". Then we got up with this guy named Walter, Brah called him "Walt Weezy" and we became cool with a guy named Willie. We called ourselves "The Team''. One of our traditions in high school was we use to take chicks home and run a train on them. The thing we use to do was send the sweetest talking guy on the team to go in first to get the girl naked and fuck her. When he was finished with her, the next guy would go in the room while she is still naked. If she goes (agrees), well, onto the next guy. If she does not go, we would put her out and make her walk home, not caring how far she lived. A couple of girls told us the word around school was "The Team" picks up bitches and running a train on them". Some girls went and some girls did not. The girls that went, I do not know if they knew about us or not. I am just going to go with they did know. Sometimes we would get a girl that wanted to get the train ran on her. We use to keep this one guy around us just because he had bitches. His name was Patrick. He use to bring over a lot of girls and we did not know how he did it. He dressed bummy. I am talking about dirty; you will look at this guy and be like why a girl would ever touch him. One day he came over to the house and he brought two white girls with him. He pulled two 40 ounces of beer out of his coat and one of the white girls asked if we had a camera. She wanted to make a porno. We called the team over and we fucked the shit out of them all night. Then one of the girls came back the next day-- the one that wanted to do the porno. My big brother, Patrick, and I ran her in. Then our Weed Man came over. We told him that he could go in and fuck her too. When he got finished, he came out breathing all hard and sweating. We asked him what was wrong. He said "nothing, just got finished fucking that bitch" Then we go in and she said that he raped her. He said "no I didn't this bitch is lying. Y'all gotta let this bitch know that when y'all bring bitches over I fuck and when I bring bitches over y'all fuck". We had to let him know "look, nigga we don't bring bitches over here so you can rape them. If she doesn't want to fuck you, she doesn't have to fuck you. We don't have time to be going down for some shit you done did". Then she said, "That's okay it ain't like he took my virginity and it ain't like this the first time this happened to me". She got very drunk that night and when everybody got finished fucking her, Patrick just left her at our house and she took off walking, stumbling away drunk. So I went looking for her and I found her lying on the school stairs crying. I walked her back down to my house and brought her into my room. My mom heard her crying so I told my mom what happened to her. My mom said "y'all be bringing all these girls to this house and you and all yo guys be fucking them. I don't see why these girls be letting y'all do this shit to them" My mom told me ''look, she can't stay here so you have to get her a cab home" so I did and my mom said she was going to cuss Rob out when she saw him. That is when Brah gave him a nickname; double R or "Rob the rapists" In school, my guys knew me as the "Weed Man". I used to give all my guys Jabs. My Jabs would be six bags of weed. They would bring me $50 and they keep

$10. I had four of the guys on the team selling weed for me and sometimes they would make at least $200 a day. I remember the first week I started to sell weed-- I was so excited from the money that I made I went and showed my mom how much I made in a week. When I showed her the money she said "boy, where did you get all that money?" and I said" from selling weed. I had been buying it from Rob. I was making more money from selling weed then selling dope in Chicago (In Chicago I would make $25 a day) Making money--that's what made me feel good about selling drugs. When I went back to school a guy tried to take some weed from little Tray. I got the team together and we had to go check him and let him know that was my weed. His name was Dave. He went and got his guys, Jeff, Calvin, Big face, and Vernon. We got into an argument but they were not doing anything but wolfing. They did not want to fight. A couple of days after that, Brah got up with this guy in one of his classes. The guy told him that he had a gun for sale. We got up with him before school and I bought it from him. He sold it to me for a quarter of weed and $75. The next day I woke up before my brother; I jumped out of bed put my clothes on for school. That morning I went downstairs and put the gun under the hood of the car that my mom just bought. The day started with me just trying to showing off the car. Then, I saw the guys that I got into it with at school. They saw me too. I noticed one of them had a little mini bat pointing at me. I pulled over in the parking lot across the street from the school and I popped the hood. I pulled the gun out and cocked it back. A couple of people was like "he got a gun" and they took off running. A big crowd of them stayed, one girl named Shatara was like "you better not shoot me" and I said, "Bitch, you better get out the way then". It was another crowd of kids behind me just getting off the bus, there was a teacher there (in the crowd) that took the bus with them. She saw me with the gun so I put the gun back under the hood and drove back home. If it were not for that teacher being out there, I would have shot one of them goofy ass boys. That is the only thing that stopped me. I walked back to school by myself because Brah had to go take a driver's test to get his license. My mom would not let us drive the car without our licenses. As soon as I walked in the school they jumped up talking GD (Fake Gangster Disciples) this and GD that. I said 'man, fuck GD you bitch ass nigga's ain't gon do shit'' The security guards grabbed me and took me to the office. As I was going to the office and I saw Big Face, he was talking crazy but he did not want to run up to do anything. I told that nigga "yeah you know what it is, run up on me, I ma beat yo big bitch ass". He kept walking and the security took me into the principal's office. The principal told me ever since I came to the school I had been causing nothing but trouble, gang banging, and a lot of other stuff. He told me that I needed to keep all that gang banging outside of the school. The principal asked me "what is your next class" and I told him "gym". He gave me a pass and told me to get on to class. I walked down to the gym and when I got there; Dave, Vernon, Calvin, and Jeff were in the locker room. One of them pulled the gates closed and said, "Where yo gun at now?" I said, "It's put up, but it can come back out at any time". One of them told me to fight Dave one on one. I told them "look it ain't going to be no one on one once y'all see me whoopin his ass. Y'all gonna jump me, anyway. Gon do what y'all gon do cause once y'all jump me-- y'all might as well not even come back to school cuz I ma kill one of you niggas!" I put my back against a locker because Vernon tried to walk up on the side of me and snake me. Therefore, I pushed him. A couple of guys stepped in front of them that were from Chicago. I did not know them they just knew I was from Chicago. I did not even hang out with them in school but they told them "I'm not about to let y'all push on big homie". As soon as they told them that (I do not know how my guys heard about it) two of my guys busted in the locker room, it was Willy and his cousin. We called him "Big Guy" he just transferred to the school from Detroit. Well they bust in the locker room and we started the fight with them. I told them "shit now it's a fair fight". We only threw a couple of punches until the security came and broke it up. The principal came and grabbed me. I body slammed him and told him "man don't put yo fucking hands on me, you see these nigga coming after me, that's when niggas get free hits and shit… you better grab one of them" I left the school and went home, by the time I got there my big brother was at home. He had his license so we went back up to the school in our car, when we got there the security guard stopped us at the door, and took us to the office. When we got to the office we talked to the principal and he was telling me "how he should have me locked up for slamming him". I was suspended for a 10-day period, so they could see what they were going to do with me or if they want me to continue going to the school. We were sent home, as we were walking out of the office it was a police officer standing outside of the door. The police officer took us to our car; and searched it. The teacher that saw me with the gun told the principal. Funny enough, the principal did not mention that to me. He was afraid that I would catch him after school and give him a "blanket party" I already put the gun under my mattress, so when they searched the car they could not find it. They trailed us home, so they could search the house. They asked us if our mom was at home. We told them "no". He asked us to call her, we did. When we talked to her, she was really pissed that she had to leave work. When she got to the house she said "boy, it better not be no fucking gun off in my house; knowing I'm on fucking parole!" She gave the police permission, to search the house. I was scared that he was going to find the gun. The police officer told us "one of y'all is coming with me". My big brother nudged me with his shoulder saying, "You go". I was sweating hard as ever! He started to search the room and he asked me "where is the gun" so I pulled out a rifle BB gun and he said, "No, that's not the gun. They said it was a little black gun". He started to look around the room again, he looked in my dresser drawers and he found some baggies and a couple of bags of weed. He said, "Now I see who's been selling weed in the school" he closed the draw and said, "I'm not here for that" Then he started back looking for the gun. He looked up at the pictures on our wall of me and my brother posing, holding the gun. He said, "Y'all have a gun, so just tell me where it's at". He went over to my bed and looked down at the mattress. My heart started beating fast…he lifted the mattress up. All I saw was a gun print. I was like "thank God" when we left out of the room and went back downstairs, the officer told my mom "your boys have a gun, they have it hidden somewhere, you need to tell them to get rid of it before it gets you into trouble". When the police left, I told my brother "man, I was so scared I thought he was going to find the gun", I asked my brother "what did you do with the gun?" He told me where he moved it to. We had shelves over our beds in the room; it was a bunch of teddy bears on the shelves. He told me he put the gun behind the teddy bears. So, while the police were searching, the gun was right over their heads. As soon as I got back upstairs I took the pictures off the wall and ripped them up. Well, they kick me out of school and I had to go to a school called Douglas. That is when I got up with my guys Percy and Brandon. I guess this is the school where all the bad kids go. It looked like a little Prison. It had an office that was full of police officers. I had to ride the little yellow school bus.

The first time I met Bethany

One day I had my eyes on this girl, her name was Bethany. What attracted me to her was--she got in an argument with a boy in school; he called her a "bitch" and she jumped across the lunchroom table, on his ass. I looked at her like man she is feisty; straight go getter, and she's pretty—that is my kind of girl. When she came back to school from being suspended, I approached her and asked her out but she told me she had a boyfriend. One day, Percy told me, "I have a girl that wants to come home with us after school!" Percy and I waited outside of the school. Percy pointed "there she goes right there" and I told him "man, I tried to holler at her a couple days ago, and she told me she has a boyfriend. Man, she ain't going" He said, "yes she is. Watch this". He went over to talk to her and she walked home with us. She was telling us how her boyfriend cheated on her and she is not fucking with him anymore. When we got to the house, the team was already there even Rob. Rob went in the room first and came back out in like 5 minutes; then I went, and she was still naked. She was about to put her clothes back on but I whipped out my dick and she just started sucking it. I pulled a condom out of my draw and fucked her. After we got finished, I ask her if she wanted to go home. She told me "no" We kicked it for a little while. She ended up changing her mind and we dropped her off at home.

Highway Robbery

One day my guys Walt Weezy and Alley Cat came in the house dancing, jumping around with weed plants/trees. My little nigga Percy and I found out that they got the plants from Williamsville Illinois where there was a big field of weed growing. After school, we got on our bikes and got on the highway. We rode our bikes all the way to Williamsville, we looked around a little bit then we came across these train tracks. It was like weed heaven. There were weed plants everywhere. Percy had a big gym bag and I had just a regular book bag. We stuffed so much weed in those bags it was ridiculous. We jumped on our bikes, got back on the highway, and were headed back to Springfield. We saw a state trooper bust a u-turn. I told Percy as he was pulling us over if he searched us and found the weed just tell him that it all belongs to me. The trooper got out of the car and said to us "don't y'all know that it is dangerous to ride bicycles on the highway". He talked to us for a minute then he tried to get us to sit in his car but, I told him "nawl we cool" because I did not want him to smell the weed. He asked us "what are you guys doing on the highway riding your bicycles anyways?" I have always been a quick thinker so I told him "my girlfriend had just recently moved to Williamsville and I just had to see her". He had me call my uncle Steve then he insisted that we sit in the car and get away from the road. I told him no again then Percy and I stood in the grass. Thank god my uncle pulled up and the state trooper didn't even search us. That was a blessing *God has plans for me*. It was a drought on weed that summer in Springfield. I made so much money that summer selling backyard boogie. I took my brother shopping. Brah talked me into buying jumpsuits. The one I bought for me was all burnt orange and the one I bought for him it was all baby blue. We looked like two fat pimps from Detroit, I regret wearing that shit now.

Tupac's back

Percy had like 10 pounds of weed and he fucked it all up when he put embalming fluid on it. Our stay at Father's building complex finally came to an end. We had to move because Father was getting sick; he was giving the business to one of his relatives. About a month before that, my mom met this guy name Bill. He was a white guy and I did not like him, because I was not raised around white people. My mama was locked up for almost five years and out for one year, when she met Bill. Within the first week or so, she moved into the downstairs apartment with him. She left the upstairs apartment to my brothers and me. Sometimes we'd see her and she'd have a crazy look in her face like she was high. I hated that look. So one day we saw a guy leaving from the basement and all of the sudden it hit me—she was back on that shit. My brothers and I blamed it on Bill. I was outside in the hall one day talking to Percy and Brandon, outside of my Uncle Steve's door. I was telling them how Bill got my mom back smoking that shit. Uncle Steve opened his door and asked me to step in. His girlfriend was white and he said "don't be taking bad about Bill; you don't know him, get to know him, that's your mom's business". Eventually I got over it I just said to myself "Steve's right; it's her life she can do what she wants". We finally moved out the building into a house on North grand, across the street from Lanphier High school. And she let Bill move in with us. One day we woke up and our Nintendo 64, all of our games, and our TV was gone. Bill was gone too. So we went looking for him. My brothers and I went over to the old apartment building and went down into the basement.

There was this hype that we knew; we called him Tupac, because he would always rap all of Tupac's songs. He was from Nigeria and he had only one leg. Tupac use to sleep in the basement from time to time. We went down to the basement and there was only a bed and a blanket down there. I yelled "Tupac, you down here?" He replied "ya" We walked over to the bed and asked Tupac "have you seen Bill's bitch ass?" He replied "nawl" but something sounded strange about Tupac's voice. He usually sounded like he was straight from Africa. Brah pointed to the bed and whisper to me "that's not Tupac". I snatched the sheets off him and it was Bill pretending to be Tupac! I kicked him, telling him "man get yo bitch ass up" and " where is our shit" he replied "what shit" I said "motha fucka you know what the fuck we talking about". Brah hit him in the eye and a little red not popped up instantaneously. We both go in on him; I mean we beat his ass. Then he ran out of the basement; we caught him in the middle of the street, and sat him on the curb. Brah hit him in the eye again! Then the red knot turned dark purple. I asked him again "where is our shit?" he says "I don't know what y'all are talking about". This guy in an 18 wheeler pulls up and gets out and ask us "what's the problem". We told him "he stole our shit and we trying to get it back from him". Bill says, "I don't know what they are talking about". Brah hit in the eye again! Now the purple knot burst open (pusch) and blood went everywhere. 18-wheeler buddy said "hold on wait one darn minute. I'm not going to sit here and watch y'all beat on this man" I said "well get the fuck back in your truck and get the fuck on". He says, "No I'm just going to call the police". I said "well call them bitch, he's the one who is going to jail for stealing our shit". He called the police. When the police got there, my mom was just coming from around the corner, walking from the house. The police officer had Bill in the car with him; the officer was talking to him about what happened. They sat there for a minute then the officer got out of his car. He and said "Bill told me he took your things: look this is what I'm going to do. Y'all gave him a pretty good ass whoopin so I'm either going to take both of y'all to jail or y'all can just let it go". I did not want to go to jail so I told the officer "it's cool we gon let it go".

Stick Bamdit

Later that year I was talking to my mom and putting my order in for Thanksgiving dinner. She knows I love strawberry cheesecake so, one morning Brandon, Percy, and I were walking to school together. Brandon says, "I don't want to go to school today" I said, "me either". Percy say "I've got to go to school my mom say she gon fuck me up of I miss another day so I'm taking my ass to school". Brandon and I walked Percy half way to school. Brandon said, "My mom's at work lets go to my house". We got over to his house. We were sitting there smoking weed while he was getting his cat high. Then he showed me this big ass gun; it was a 45, he told me it was his grandpa gun. We did not have any money that day that is all I had were six bags of weed. I told him that if we did make any money off the weed I could not spend it because I had to re cop, to buy another half. I told him "I know how to make fake dope". He asked me how so I told him "we need some baking soda, oral gel, and yellow candle wax". We made some and it looked like the real thing. Brandon told me he knows exactly where to get it off at. We had to catch the bus to the east side. While we were leaving the house, I said, "Why don't we take the gun with us". We grabbed the gun; we left the house, and got on the bus, As soon as we got to the back of the bus Brandon took the gun out and started twirling it around and cocked it back. I tell him "look, you damn dummy don't you see this bus has cameras on it". So, I told him to put the gun up. When we got off the bus, he took me to a guy's house that smokes crack. When we got there, the guy asked to try a little piece. I let him try it and his pipe turned black and white at the top. He told me that he would buy some but it has too much baking soda on it. We left his house and starting walking around the east side. We ran into another guy that Brandon knew. Brandon told this guy that I have some weed and some crack and the guy asked me if he could see the crack. He stuck his finger in the bag and tasted it; it took a while for the oragel to hit him. However, when it did hit him, he shook his head up and down, and said, "That's that shit"! He took me to this house and it looked abandoned. He knocked on the door and pretended to talk to someone. Then, we went to another house, and he told me "wait in the garage". He went into the house, and he came back out asking, "How much weed do you have?" I told him "5 bags". Then I put it in his hand. Then, he asked, "How much work do you have?" I told him "I have a couple 50 pieces". He asked to see it, and then out of nowhere he asked, "How much money do you have in your pocket?" I asked, "Why the FUCK you wanna know". He said "you know what this is" grabbing at his waist "Low that shit" I said "What the fuck is you talking about, it ain't shit" As I pulled the 45 off my hip, cocking it back". Brandon walked in the garage. I said, "Put my shit back in my hand". His eyes got big as fuck. He was scared as shit at this time: begging and pleading for me not to shoot him. So I told Brandon "see what the fuck is in his pants". Brandon searched him and pulled a big ass stick out. I said, "Look, goofy ass dude I just almost blew your fucking brains out, over a stick". I got my shit back from the "stick mugger" and Brandon and I walked away. As we got two blocks up, a police car pulled behind us. The car turned on its light. The officer says from his intercom "Stop, turn around and put your hands up". We started walking with our backs turned to the police car, I tell Brandon "I have everything on me; how about you take off running and let them chase you, so I can walk away". This goofy tells me "my boots ain't tied" I said "I got your granddaddy's gun on me, just take off running" Now what I should have done is thrown his granddaddy's gun at him! But, I say fuck it and take off running. Brandon's bitch ass causally walks off and they did not even chase him. I asked him to do that for me and, he played me. While I am running, I run past a dumpster, it rips my coat off, spins me in a circle, and I fall. It is the same-burnt orange jumpsuit jacket that my brother tricked me into buying. I got up, took off running and got to an ally. I threw the gun over a fence and ran around a garage. I saw the police right behind me and I tried to run another lap around the garage. The officer got smart, stopped and I tried to run right past him, but the son of a bitch jumped on my back. I go down face first in a puddle of mud. The officer puts his knee in my neck and my face is all in the mud; He yelled at me "now look at this shit, you got me all muddy, and all I wanted to do was talk!" He put the handcuffs on me, told me to get on my knees. He picked me up and as he was taking me to his car: guess who was walking up the street? The stick bandit! As he was walking up, he pointed at me saying "that's the guy who robbed me; he took my phone and all of my money!" I said, "That mother fucker tried to rob me!" They searched my pockets, found MY phone and no money. They took my phone and gave it to him. As it turns out, I was robbed anyways…by the fucking police! The block is full of officers now; they are looking in the dumpster, because they must have thought I threw something in there. I was searched at his car. The weed and the fake dope fell right out of my pants leg. I could not believe all that fucking running I was doing and it did not fall until I got to his damn car. The officer and I both saw it fall. I say to him "shit, it ain't mine!" He said, "I just saw it fall from your pants, it's yours". I told him "no, it's not!" He hurled me into the car and took me down to the station. They called my mom and told me all I have to do is tell, whose gun it is and I can go home. I said "mom, I don't know what they are talking about". My mom said "boy, its thanksgiving you better tell 'em whose gun it is so you can go home". I stuck to my story: then I spent the next 6 months in juvie.

Juvie Stint

I was 15 at this time and I was full of a lot of anger. When I first arrived at the juvenile detention center, it felt like I was at the nut house, all over again. I was trapped. Most of the time I spent confined to my cell; we would be locked down. I had to get thru this stint. I was sad because I had to spend the holidays locked up and alone. Most people would have told but, I am not that dude to tell; I was not raised like that. One day I was sitting down writing a letter and a guy named Marcus came over to me, and tried to read it. We get into it! (I was unsure about my reading and writing abilities) I pushed him away from me. The security guard catches us, and breaks it up before we actually start fighting. They then locked us down in our room. Marcus's cell was right next to mine and he was talking shit to me. He was woofing for the whole two- three hours they had us locked down. As soon as they let us out, I sat down on the couch to watch TV. Marcus came up behind me and hit me in my jaw. I instantly jumped up and squared up with him, I ran up on him, hit him, that is when his guy Bruno came out of nowhere, and started woofing. I grabbed a chair and got to swinging it. Neither of them wanted to run up but then security broke it up. There was this kid named Skylar and he got into with Bruno, shortly after I had the little scuffle with Bruno. Skylar and Bruno were both from Decatur and they were already beefing before they got to juvie. The juvenile center was set up into pods. Each pod has its own lunchroom. Skylar went to put his lunch tray up; Bruno walked out of his pod's lunchroom, behind Skylar and grabbed him by his neck. Skylar was trying to get up but Bruno was holding him down by the back of his neck and punching him in the face! Skylar was looking at me with the saddest fucking face ever, looking like "help me". He actually said the words "Pig, help me". So, I look back at him like "shit, I ain't got anything to do with that". Bruno is a fucking monster and way bigger than the security guards are. So one of the security guards picked Bruno up and slammed him so hard...That his leg broke and I heard the nastiest snap ever! The security guard was still wrestling while Bruno's leg was dangling. Bruno let out the most painful scream that I had ever heard in my entire life. The security guard finally came to his senses and realized what happened. He should have never slammed him like that. I think the security guard tried to make an example out of him.

In the meantime--Between time

Three weeks later, I got a visit from Brah and Alley cat. They both come in smelling like weed heavily. We sit down and talk. Brah pulls out $200-300. He tells me "Brah, do you know our $5 rocks in Chicago, goes for $20 here in Springfield." I say, "Get the fuck out of here!"
That is when I decided to get into the Game...
I went to court and my public defender told me; they would drop the armed robbery charge (me "robbing" the stick bandit), if I admitted the gun belonged to me (it did not), and they will let me out today on probation. I said "shitttt! Where do I sign?" I got out that day. I get to the house and Brah told me "Man, I couldn't wait for you to get home, man". "Mom put me out and made me sleep in the car because I wouldn't give her all

my work. Every time I gave her a $20 bag, she said she would pay me tomorrow, but then she came and asked for another one. She said it made her throat hurt and it was it was some bullshit. Give her another bag. I say no and she throws me out the house. Then I'd go and get a hype rental and my BM (his pregnant girlfriend) and I would have to sleep in the car."

    I started selling drugs and we put our money together. We planned to save our money to move out. Now that I am out, I am going through the same shit my brother was going through. Now she wants me to give her my work or she will put me out. We did not know anything about grams, balls, and quarters. We would give Alley cat our money to get us work. But, he was cheating us. We would give him $125 and he would bring us two grams (It should have been 3.5 grams) One day Brah bought a 1986 Monte Carlo from a hype. He drove it for maybe a week and it broke down on him. One of the other guys we kicked it with name was Mac; he was a stick up man. He wanted to buy Brah's car. Brah sold it to him. For a Mossberg shotgun, a 22, and 200 bucks.

For the Love of Guns

We had the shotgun for like two-three weeks. We already tested the 22. It was this big tree in our back yard. Brah did not want to shoot the gun. We had 30-40 shotgun shells. One night around 3 am, I decided to try it out. It was pouring down rain that night. I told Brah I am about to go in the back and shoot the shotgun to see if it works. My mom and little Brah were both asleep in the house. I went to the back door, cocked it, and as soon as a big Thunder hit. I shot the gun, "Boom". My mama woke up instantly "boy, what the fuck is y'all doing out there?" I says "Nothing mom it's the Thunder". "Boy that ain't no God Damn thunder, y'all better stop playing with them guns". Another Thunder clapped and I shot it again" Boom". I ran in the house excited. Our next gun we bought was a Chinese AK 47. It has two 50 clips and 100 round drum roll. Rob sold it to us. It came with 300 bullets. We were into with the outlaws. One day we were on 7th Street and Jeff came riding up the street, bumping his Music. I jumped off the porch with a 13 shot 22. I fired all 13 shots at him. All I saw was sparks bouncing off his car and hitting his windows. When I shot his car up, I did not know he had his baby in the car with him. Later on that night, he came back and they shot 444's sister Shameka's apartment up. We saw Jeff a week later parked across from my house in the school parking lot. We send our guy Willie across the street and he threw an AK bullet on his lap and said, "See if you catch the next one". He jumped out the car and said, "So that's what we on!" Brah says "nigga, play with it".

Life on 7th Street was crazy. We had like five to six houses to run too. My big brother and I made it like a battlefield over there when we came through. If you did not stay on the block, you could not play on the block. We made this our own Little "ChIraq" I was 16 at the time and big Brah was 18, my Little brother never hung around us he stayed in school. He used to always tell us y'all stupid I will never be like y'all-- which was selling drugs and smoking weed: banging and gun slanging all day… that was our life.

It had been a year since I was kicked out of Lanphier and I attended Douglas. I was coming home from school one day and I saw Vernon he was like "Pig, what's up man smoke somethin". I looked at Brah and said "what the fuck this nigga doing over here? Watch this, Brah" I had on tight ass school uniform pants so I had to skip over to him. I skipped towards him and hit him right in the mouth and asked him "what the fuck you doing over here?" We got to boxing and I am beating his ass, then Brah comes from nowhere. Vernon saw him so he tried to run but when he turned around to run but Brah football tackled him into a parked car and broke his thumb. I told him" I better not catch you on this side no mo'" A couple months later, I walked my girlfriend to work and on my way back I ran into little Tray. He was asking about some work and telling me "there is a guy in the house that just got out of jail; he is a part of the outlaws". He came outside and asked me if my name was Pig? I told him "yes, what's good?" Then he asked me "you supposed to be into it with the outlaws"? I said "yes" He said, "well, I'm an outlaw and you ain't into it with me". I told him "if you an outlaw I'm into it with you too then, Nigga" little Tray told me to just walk off. I told little Tray "if he walks off that porch I'm gon change his life for him". Little Tray ran up on the porch and told him something and he turned around and went back into the house. I walked off and got like three blocks up the street and I ran into Vernon. He said, "Yes, I caught yo bitch ass now" I guess he thought I was going to bitch up. I got my gun on me but I did not let him know that so I take my phone off my hip and sit it on the curb and through my hands up with him. As I moved towards him, he moved back and it went on like that for like a minute or two. I told him "man, I'm not about to be chasing you" I picked up my phone and told him "this ain't what you want, you a bitch and you know it". I walked off thinking about shooting him in his head. Then, I thought to myself he is not even worth it.

Snitches get Stitches

We got into it with these goofies from around the corner for trying to hustle in our neighborhood. We had to let them know that "they had to move around". They tried to get tough so we had to bring the toys out! One day I saw a car trying to creep up through the alley across the street from us. I grabbed my 17 shot 9mm, ran across the street, and lay down in the bushes and waited to see what they were going to do. They dropped off one guy, so as he got closer to me I popped up out of the bushes, asked him "what the fuck you doing up in my alley!" He said, "I'm looking for my phone". But I recognized him; he was one of the guys from around the corner. I pointed my gun at him and pulled the trigger but my gun was on safety. I took it off safety and shot seven times. I had him hopping around like a bunny rabbit! I tried to kill that boy! I ran into 444 sister's house, across the street and watched out the Window. The block filled up with police cars. I watched the police go door to door asking questions. The only person that came out to talk was the neighborhood mechanic, John. Everything happened behind his house. The next day, big Brah's name was in the papers. The mechanic told the police Brah's name; said that he was behind his house; he let off 5 to 8 shot, and said nobody was harmed only a dog was killed. I politely walked across the street; knocked on the mechanics door, walked in, hit him in his shit and beat the fuck out of him. I broke his alarm clock across his head, pushed his TV down on him, and drug him through his house. I told him "if I ever catch you talking to the police about anything that happens on this block again, I'm gon come over here and kill you, bitch"

Brah's Side Chick/Our Chick

My brother and I were just moving out of my mom house. I got into it with Mac, we use to be cool until he found out my brother was fucking his girl, Vodka. Ok Vodka was the town freak and she was Brah Little side chick. When Brah heard about Mac, cuffing her he had a talk with him; he told him "man, she ain't no wifey material". Mac went right on ahead and cuffed her anyway. But that did not stop Brah from fucking her. Brah gave her the nickname "Vodka" I guess because he could take a shot of that ass whenever he wanted. Vodka is a light-skinned chick, thick as hell. She is pretty until she opens her mouth. She says the craziest shit. She is that girl you can hear a block up and around the corner and you know it is her because the shit that comes out of her mouth. One day Mac was locked up but Brah and I did not know. Vodka came over to the house; she had some work she wanted to get off and she was over our house fucking on Brah. When Brah's BM came in the house I would act like Vodka was there with me. Brah Brought one of his guys down here from the city, Maine. One day he had to go back to Chicago, to go court, and Vodka wanted to go with us to go shopping. Actually, that is when I found out she was selling Mac's work to get him out of jail. I let her go to Chicago with me (Brah stayed at the crib to make some money) as soon as we got there; we got on Cicero Street, my brother's front axle broke, on his car. Maine and I pushed the car to a nearby ally. Maine called somebody to come pick him up, so he could get to court. He left us in the alley for hours. He came back with a tow truck then took us to a shop to get the car fixed. After that, we went to the mall. Vodka bought a hoe fit. Vodka bought this little ass skirt, high heels, and some thongs. She spent Mac's money that she was supposed to use to bond him out of jail. Maine dropped us off at a hotel; he went and got us a couple bags of weed. There was a liquor store on the side of the hotel and a soul food restaurant across the street. We went to the soul food restaurant and got something to eat. She said "I feel like getting' fucked up, let's get something to drink". We walked over to the liquor Store to get something to drink. Back at the room, we were drinking, smoking, and she was telling me how my brother does not treat her the way I treat her. She said "I want to tell you something, but I think you're gonna tell yo' brother". I said, "No, I'm not" she said, "I like you, Pig". I said," I like you too, you cool". She said "not like that. I like you in a different way". I said, "Hell nawl, I ain't going! I can't do that to Brah" She said "see, I knew you was gonna tell," I said "I'm not gon tell, it's just I can't do it". She went to take a shower and I was drunk as hell, so I lay down to go to sleep. She walked out of the bathroom ass hole naked. I mean that body was looking good! I did not know what else to do. I tried not to look at her but she just kept staring at me. She said, "You mean to tell me you don't want this pussy, Pig," I said "fuck it, I'll be right back". I ran next door to the liquor store and grabbed some condoms. I got back to the room and beat that pussy up! I woke up that next morning, she was naked, and that pussy was just staring at me so I beat that pussy up again! Maine called "get up and call to check on the car, it should be ready. I'm on my way to get y'all". Maine walked into the room and saw all the empty liquor bottles. He turned to me, and asked me "was she good to you, Pig?" All I could do is smile. Vodka came out of the bathroom and smiled. Maine said "y'all ass is crazy, come on lets go". On our way out the door-- all the liquor we had leftover, Vodka just got to downing it. I told her "it's too early to be getting drunk and it's about to get hot outside". She did not care. When I saw Vodka buy the hoe fit, I assumed she had bought it to wear to the club. But, she put that shit on for the day. She had her ass cheeks hanging all out the bottom of her skirt. She kept trying to pull it down to keep all that ass in. We went to pay for the car then we went up to the mall. We got some more weed and we smoked a blunt. We walked around the mall for a little bit and that is when the liquor really hit her. She told me she was feeling sick and she wanted to go sit in the car. She starts throwing up. I was too embarrassed; it looked like I was with a prostitute-- from the outfit, to the throwing up. I said "I told you not to drink all of that shit". What made it worse, Brah did not have A/C in his car. I went and got her a mystic pop. We picked up Maine and hit the road. As soon as we got home, she said she was still hungover and tired. She asked if she could sleep it off in my bed. I told her "hell nawl, we gon get caught". But I ended up letting her do it anyways, even though' I was afraid to get caught by Brah. She slept for a little while then she woke up and called my name. I went into the room and she asked me if I still had that last condom. I said, "Yes, I still got it but we can't fuck here, you have to wait". She said "it's cool, we ain't gon get caught" She lifted the sheets up and she was naked. We got to fucking again. The next thing you know I heard Brah walked in the house. He called out "Brah, Brah". I got off her. He knocked on my bedroom door. He did not wait for me to say come in, he just busted in. Vodka got under the covers. He said" I see why yo ass ain't up yet, you got one of yo freaks up in here". Then Vodka pops from up under the covers and said, "G.M.B, G.M.B bitch, keep it in the family, Hug", Brah ran out the house dying laughing. It is funny because I thought he would be mad. Later on that day, I smashed one more time then sent her home. Little did she know somebody bonded Mac out of jail? She called me at 2 or 3 am, she said "Pig" then I heard someone say, "Give me the fucking phone" it was Mac! He said "all this time I been thinking Yo brother's been fucking my bitch. All along, it has been you… its cool. Well I just beat our bitch's ass. She told me everything…So you took our bitch to the city, huh Maine? Shopping and all the shit". I told him "look man, I didn't buy yo bitch shit! That was yo money she spent!" He went back to beating her ass. About an hour later Mac showed up at my house! I woke Brah up; I grabbed two of my guns out of the heating vent. I passed the 9 mm to Brah and I grabbed my Dirty Harry. I opened the door and we pointed our guns at him. It was some out the movies type shit, like off "Bad Boys". He said, "What's all of this for, Maine". I asked him "WHAT THE FUCK YOU DOING AT MY HOUSE" He said, "Our bitch said she left my scale over here, Maine". I said "yo bitch ain't leave shit over here so you better get the fuck off my porch, before I stop yo' engine, MAINE" He said "Ok" with a mug on his face, as he walked away.

Indictments

From the little situation with Vodka, made the beef with Mac get heavy. We left 7th street alone because all of the guys moved off the block. Some new dudes, from Mississippi moved over there, they were cool with Mac…I guess they were his little workers. We gave 7th Street up because Brah and I had a $100,000 spot on, 9th Street. We were making $2 to 3000 daily. Mac told his little' workers that we were into with him; one of Mac's main guys that he kicked it with, was this nigga named, Blue. One day I was riding up 7th Street; Blue stopped and folded his arms and mean mugged me. I guess it was because I was shinin' harder than them niggas. They were all powder snorters, on some hating shit. I let him get away with it once. The second time, I had to stop and say something. I backed my car up; jumped out and asked him "what's good, nigga you got a problem with me?" He just kept his arms folded and stared at me. I told him "this ain't what you want; yo money ain't long enough to war with me." I jumped back in to my car and peeled off. I went and told Brah what happened. Brah and I went and made a run somewhere. When we got back, the upstairs neighbor told us to come up stairs and looked at this whole in his wall. He told us: someone shot the house up, if he or his girl were sitting there on the phone, that the bullet could have hit either one of them in the head. That is when; we noticed that our crib had been shot up. We talked to another neighbor and they told us-- that some dudes came up the alleys, with black garbage bags, pulled guns out of them, and shot up the house. I know they saw that our cars were not in the driveway…My brother's BM and his son was there they were in the tub. There were buckshot's, from a shotgun, right outside the bathroom window. They did not go through the house. Brah, Maine, and I were sitting in the backyard talking about what we should do. I told them "you already know what I'm ready to do, I'm ready to kill something" Brah and Maine, told me we have to do this smarter than that. They wanted us to go over there and talk first. I said "fuck talking; I'm takin' my thumper with me". Brah said "we not taking any guns, we just going to talk". Brah and Maine walked over there. I jumped in Brah's car and drove. Brah and Maine were walking too slow. I went up the street without them. I got up to the house and jump out and said "what's good, you niggas want to shoot at my house? Nigga shoot at me. That house ain't gon shoot back!" I swung at the closest nigga that was by me. He ducked and pulled out a gun. I told him "you ain't gon use it". One of his guys said to him "put the gun down and box him" He said "I'm not about to fight that big nigga". I got back into the car and went to the crib. I got my Dirty Harry. I parked in the back of the snitch-ass-mechanics house. I ran through the gangway; Brah and Maine were out there talking to them. I pointed the gun and said, "Fuck all that talking!" Brah said, "Don't shoot!" Two of the guys pulled out guns and ran to the back of the house. I didn't shoot because Brah was over there in the way. He told me "it is too many people out here, do not shoot". We went back home and talked about it… The plan was to catch them at night, when there was nobody around to witness it. But, that next day indictments came out. Brah, Maine, and I sat on the front porch and watched the police jump out of minivans wearing mask. We are from Chicago and we never saw anything like this! I left and went to go do something and when I came back my brother's BM told me that the police just picked up Brah and Maine. I thought about it, and said to myself "we were all on the indictment list". So I waited until nighttime to go back to the house. I went in through the back door to grab all of my things; I grabbed my guns, my money, my clothes, and dope. My brother's BM, my BM (pregnant), and I got ready to leave. When we were on our way out the door, I saw four or five police officers coming up to knock! I just sat on the couch and contemplated about what I was going to do. I just sat there and let them knock. We waited for the police to leave. We saw, officer "Frankie", the well-known town cop. Frankie was sitting' on my porch swing; swinging back and forth, I assume he was waiting on a search warrant. The rest of the officers were sitting on the side of my house. I was pacing back and forth; I did not know what to do. I told my baby mama and Brah's baby mama to grab the guns and the dope, and run across the alley to Donnie's house. I still had two "Dillinger's" downstairs in the basement, but I was not worried about them. I grabbed the money and some clothes. I was about to run out the back door but a police officer drove across the alley. I almost was caught, that scarred the shit out of me. After they rode past--I took off running to Donnie's house. Then I went over to my BM's house… she was 3 month pregnant with my son. I hid out at her house for almost 2 months. One day I said, "Fuck it" I have to get out this house. I said to myself "I would rather turn myself in, than to stay around this crazy ass family. Her mom would always make these little sideways comments, I just could not take it anymore. I just bought a car that I had never even driven yet. I went and got my license, plates, and my insurance. While I was staying with my BM, my brother's BM did not have anywhere to stay. She stayed with my mom and her cousins from time to time. I helped her out with gas money so she could get back and forth to work. I even gave her money to keep my brother's car up and to take care of my nephew. One day 444's little' sister came to me and said, "You know your brother's baby mama down there fucking Mac, right?" Now that is fucked up! For 1.); that is the enemy! For 2.) I was just telling her to find a house; I was going to pay for it. My brothers BM came and talked to me the day after I found out that she was fucking Mac. She came to me crying; she said, "The car keeps breaking down on me, it's down the street, on a flat tire right now. I need some gas to get to work, and I miss yo brother so much" When she said that... I tried to hold it in; I was going to tell my brother about what she was doing out here in these streets. I wanted see what he wanted me to do about it. But, she pissed me off talking about how she missed Brah. I snapped and said "BITCH YOU DON'T MISS MY BROTHER! You're down there fucking that bitch ass nigga Mac". She said, "I'm not fucking anybody! Who told you that?" I said "don't worry about who told me you lying bitch! Everybody ain't lying on you. Look man, stay the fuck away from me you sleazy bitch! Do not say shit else to me. Do not ask me for shit else bitch. You are dead to me!" She walked off crying. I hid out in my BM mom's house for like two more weeks. Brah called me and I told him what has been going on with his filthy ass BM. He told me to take his car away from that bitch! I saw her and tried to take the car. She parked the car in the back of her cousin house and said she would call the police on me.

    I was driving down Enterprise St. and the police pulled me over. He asked for my license and registration. He went back to the car and ran my name. He came back and asked me to step out the car. He said "I'm gonna be straight up with you; somebody called us and said that you had a warrant and that you didn't have any license" I already knew who it was! The officer informed me that I didn't have a warrant and my license is cool *God has plans for me* The officer asked me could I follow him across the street. It was Brah's BM's cousin's house! I called my BM and told her to walk over to Rita's house. I told the police "the reason she called you guys is because my brother wanted me to get his car from her". Brah's BM came outside telling me "you're not getting shit, it's my car, because your brother left it to me". There were police officers out there that did not like me, or my brother. They ran the license plates, and saw that the car belonged to him. The next thing you know; one of the police officers came to me with a cell phone and told me that my brother wanted to talk to me! I was surprised; the police officer went through all of that trouble, to get my brother on the phone. After I talked to Brah, I gave the phone back to the police officer. He asked my brother if he wanted me to take the car. He told him them yes. The police officer told Brah's BM "well, give him the keys". She said, "So well, let me get all my shit up out of the car!" The police told me to wait out front while she got all of her shit out of the car, but they were back there too long. Therefore, I had to investigate. I got to the back yard and that bitch was taking my brother's radio and his speakers out of the car. I told the police officer "don't none of that stuff belongs to her, all of that shit in that car belongs to my brother" The police officer told her to put everything back, even her clothes, and give me the keys. If I were a dirty ass nigga, I would have told her to put the clothes back because after all, my brother did buy all that shit for the nasty bitch. But I let her take them. I was about to jump in to my brother's car, I hear her tell her my BM that she is going to whoop her ass! I told her "play with it bitch! Touch her if you want too, I'm gonna fuck you up!" I am finally free now… it is back to the money.

Surprise

    I spent a lot of money, while I was hiding out for a few months. I moved back in with my mom; it is time for me to get my money back up, now I am back on the block with the guys. I had to move my spot to 6th street, because the police shut my 9th street spot down when my brother was indicted. My moneys looking good, so I put some rims on my car. Brah was still in the county building fighting his case. While he was in the county building, I attended his court date and I found out his bond was $5,000. I also found out the reason he was arrested; he sold crack to an undercover police officer, and it was videotaped. I told him I was working on getting the $5,000 to get him out and I told him about the rims I put on my car. He wanted to see the car; he told me to bring it up to the country building around 5 p.m. I did not let him know that I had an extra surprise for him. I went and picked up Vodka and she was wearing this little ass short skirt with her ass cheeks hanging out. I pulled up to the country building and waited for Brah to come to the window. I told Vodka "get out the car and shake that ass for Brah" She pulled off her panties, jumped on the hood of my car, bent over, and gave the whole J block a show. I mean ass and pussy everywhere! I was so turned on by that shit; I took her to the crib and beat that pussy up. After I beat that shit up, I took her home… that Vodka, she is a wild girl. Now it is back to the block.

We at War over here, Homie

I was sitting on 444's sister, Shamika porch, it is a hot day. The block is doing its thing. We were all having fun and I made so much money. I was about to leave and come back after the sun went down. I was feeling good! Then here comes this bitch ass nigga Mac riding up the block. I was going to give him a pass because I was feeling so good. But he yelled out "Pig, what's up" and then this bitch ass nigga smiled at me. All I saw was red; I mean he pissed me off! I said, "444, hand me my 44" I got six shots in my 44; I held it up and pointed it at him as if I was a sharpshooter. As his car went past, the bullets were tearing patches of concrete out of the street. When I finished shooting, him or someone that was in the car with him, shot back one time. It sounded like a BB gun, we all laughed. An old white couple lived two houses down from 444's sister. They were sitting on their porch watching me the whole time I was shooting. They stood up, looked down while shaking their heads and walked in the house. The police came around asking if we heard any gunshots. We told them that we heard shots on the other block. This guy came from across the street; he asked, "Who shot back at that car?" I asked "why" he said, "let me show you my car" I walked across the street to look at his car. The bullet went through his back window; it did not shatter it, instead it melted it over. The bullet went thru the ceiling of the car and gave it a sunroof! He asked, "Who's going to pay for this?" I told him "ain't nobody paying for shit! Your car should not have been right there! We at war over here, homie!" and I walked off. That next morning I was sitting on 6th street at my mom's house; we were fixing my Bub, listening to my music, kicking it with the guys. This preacher was standing there looking at me. He would always ask me to turn my music down. I would always tell him "It's early and I can play my music. Take yo ass in the house" I would always get into with this preacher about my music. Two weeks later while at my mom's house Brah's BM came over and told me "it's Tippin' on 7th Street". It was a Sunday and I knew it was not money moving on 7th Street, especially since I moved my spot to 6th street. I already knew what she was up to. She was still fucking with Mac. Mac had to tell her to try to get me over to 7th Street. First, this bitch tried to get me locked up, now she trying to get me killed! Me being the person I am; I told my man's Jun-Jun to get the pistols together and grab my puppy. I hopped in my whip and drove over to 7th street. Jun-Jun and I were sitting in front of Mac's guy's house on the hood of my car. Jun-Jun was playing; with the puppy and every hype that walked up, fucked with me. I saw Mac's guys getting mad because I am snatching all the money that is walking up. Next thing you know, Mac pulls up with this light-skinned nigga named Ghost. They parked in the back of the house, as they walked up; I saw that they both had guns in their hands. I leaned back on the car as they approached me. Mac said to me "where the keys at" I said "keys to what" He said "give me the keys to the car" I said "the keys are in the car but y'all ain't taking shit" Mac said to the light skin nigga "get into the car". I look at Jun-Jun and said "Jun-Jun, kill both of these bitch ass niggas!" They turned around and looked at Jun-Jun, and that is when I took off running across the street. I did not have my gun on me and I needed to get out the way because I knew Jun-Jun was about to act a fool. I looked back while I was running and Mac shot at me one time. (I do not know what is up with this nigga with his onetime shooting ass) Jun-Jun tore the block up! As I looked from across the street--the light-skinned nigga jumped through my car window, and took off with my shit! I ran to Jun-Jun's crib and grabbed all the guns. We ran back to 7th Street and when we got there, the block was full of police. We turned back around and put all the guns in my BM's next-door neighbor's barbecue grill. As we walked from the side of the house, a news crew was pulling up, and all Mac's guys were still out there. All their bitches were the first to run their mouth saying that I started a gunfight. The police grabbed me, searched me, and they did not find anything. I told them "If I would've had my gun on me, you'd be picking up two dead bodies!" I also told them-- I was robbed of my car. They asked me who robbed me. I told them "I do not know who it was, and could you please find my shit". They told me that they were looking for it. I said "it looks like y'all got the whole police force on this block, how could y'all be looking for my shit?" When the police left, I told Mac's guys "y'all have to move off the block tonight!"

    A couple hours later, I got up with Jun-Jun and his girl Kathy. We ran into Tez; and drove around looking for Mac and Ghost. We rolled down every block they hung out on. We finally, ran into all of Mac's guys, they were all hanging out in their little minivan. I said, "Stop the car and let me out right here!" We all got out the car. Jun-Jun had two 22s, Tez had the nine, and I had my Dirty Harry. Jun-Jun emptied his clips, Tez only shot three times and he had a 17 shot. I do not know why he only let three goes. I think he was scared to kill somebody. When I shot my Dirty Harry: both of my guys stopped shooting and ducked down, as if somebody else was behind us shooting, because my shit was so loud! After we were done, we got back in the car with Kathy. But, as we got half way up the street, we saw Tez's brothers BM and jumped in the car with her. We put the guns under the hood of her car and she took us back out north. As soon as I got back to the crib, I took a shower, to wash the gunpowder off me. As I was getting out, I heard an aggressive knock at the door. It was the police! I thought they were there about the shooting; perhaps someone was killed, and someone told on me. But, it was about my car. They found it on the highway and they told me it was near Decatur. The radiator hose had burst. A couple of days before this happened; my mechanic told me that I needed a new radiator hose. Good thing I did not get it fixed right away. The police officer told me that if I wanted my car towed it would be $75. When the tow truck man got to my house, he told me it was $150. I did not have $150 on me, at the time. I think I only had $ 110. I argued with him at first, telling him that the police officer told me that it was going to be $75. He said, "Well, I don't know what that officer told you but it's $150" Kathy tried to write him a check for the extra $40, but he would not accept it. He jumped back into his truck and pulled off. While he was pulling off, I threw my pop at him and it burst all over his truck. Later on that night, my mom's African friend came over. I sat up all night selling her crack; she spent over $500 with me. That next morning, I went up to his shop and when I got there, my car was sitting on the inside of his garage. I walked in and tried to hand him the $150. He would not take it; he walked off and came back with some papers, with a list of shit I owed him. It listed: $35 for a car wash, $150 for the tow, and $75 for keeping it overnight—a total of $260. I put the $260 on his desk and asked him if he could take my car back to my house. He told me that I had to call another tow truck to move it, because he was not towing it. I said "that's cool, I'm about to push my shit out yo' garage!" As I was about to push my car out of his garage, he proceeded to close the garage door down on the hood of my car! I picked up a shovel in his garage and told him "if that fucking garage door touches my car I'm gon kill you in this bitch!" He lifted it back up, went into his office and called the police. When the police arrived, they told me "Mr. Jackson, it's you again. We are getting sick of your shit. All this week we've been getting calls and most of them have something to do with you". One of the police officers told me to stand across the street. I asked him "what about my car?" The officer said, "stand across the street and if you say another word to this man I'm taking you to jail" I called another tow truck company and they took my car home for me.

Fireman/You Gotta Move Tonight

Later on that night, I got on my bike, went up to the gas station with some bottles to fill with gasoline. I rode my bike to the east side; I was on my way to the house where I just shot at Mac's guys. I ran into my nigga 444 on my way over there, he said, "what sup Pig, what you on? You look like you on some bullshit". I asked him to ride with me. I told him "I am going to burn these niggas house down" He said, "boy, yo ass is crazy," I said "are you coming or not" He jumped on his bike and rode with me . I gave "4" a couple bottles and I held the rest. We ripped some t-shirts and sprinkled gasoline on them. I stuffed them into the bottles and set them on fire. We threw them at the house; they exploded, burning the house down. On my way back out north I watched fire trucks pass me by…I smelled like straight gasoline. I got home and jumped in the shower. I woke up the next morning like nothing happened. I walked on 7th Street to make sure all Mac's guys moved off the block. 444's sister told me
"you had those niggas moving all they shit out, around 3 or 4 o'clock in the morning". A week or two later, my BM and I got into it and I told her to go home. She was seven and half months pregnant. I told her I was going to watch her walk home, because she was scared to walk by herself. She was afraid that Mac was going to do something to her. I watched her as she walked across the street. She got by the 7th Street alley and I saw Mac's Tan car coming up the street. I saw the passenger side door open; his guy Blue reached out the car door, as if they were trying to kidnap her. I yelled out "you better

keep that motha fucking car moving or I'm going shoot that bitch up" I didn't have my gun on me at the time. I just said it to scare him. He ran two stop signs going up Enterprise; my nigga 4 was just walking from Jun-Jun house. He asked me what happen. I told him "them bitch ass niggas just tried to kidnapped my BM, go grab me one of my guns from Jun-Jun" He brought me back the 17 shot, 9mm" As soon as he gave it to me, Mac came riding back up the street. He slowed down coming up 6th street. While he is making a turn on Enterprise, I guess he realized that I did not have my gun on me and he came back around the block. I was standing in my mom old driveway, three houses away from the corner of Enterprise. I just moved my mom out of her apartment and into a house. Mac was driving slowly, and then he smiled at me. I opened fire; I emptied my clip trying to blow his goddamn car up! Then I walked into my mom's old apartment and put the gun under the couch. There was only a couch and a TV left in it, because I was trapping out of it. 4 told me "come on lets run to my sister's house" I was not thinking, I should have ran the other direction. But, I ran with him. We ran past the alley and ran past my BM's crib. We ran straight up 7th street. The police were right behind us and we made it to 4's sister house. The police were banging on the door. We let them in and I walked outside, they put the handcuffs on 4 and me. They put us in the car and they searched in the house, looking for the gun. One of the police officers came to the car and took me out. He told me to stand there. As I was standing by the officer's car, another police car drove by with the preacher who stayed next door to me, in the front seat! All I saw is the preacher shake his head up and down, identifying me. They took me down to the police station and sat me in the interrogation room for hours. An officer comes in the room and said, "Well, we got a search warrant for your apartment, we got a statement from the preacher next door from you, and we have your pretty ass 9mm. Now, do you care to let me know what happened?" He said, "I'm gonna read to you what the preacher from next door said about you. This is his statement:

> I know this guy; he stays next door from me. He is so disrespectful. He and his friends stay up all night playing loud music. I ask if he could please turn his music down. He says to me "hell nawl get the fuck back in the house" Today I see him walk into the middle of the street and shoot 15 to 17 times, at this brown car that was turning down Enterprise Street. Then he turned around and walked off like it was nothing, as it was an everyday life for him.

I told the officer "look man, this guy came down the block shooting at me, I shot back" I thought that by saying that, it was going to get me out of trouble. It did not; it got me in trouble. I was 17 at the time and that is when I found out, that it does not help you to talk to the police, it only fucks you! I would have known that, if they had read me my rights first. They locked me up and I had a $2000 bond. They took me across the street and put me in a cell with Tez. He told me "while the police were sitting outside yo crib waiting on a search warrant. We ran in there and walked out with the TV. One of the officers tried to come in the house; I blocked him with the TV. One of the little guys grabbed the gun and took off running with it, they didn't even catch him, and you don't have to worry about the gun," I told Tez "man, I fucked up! They told me they had the gun and the preacher next door from me made a written a statement against me, saying that he saw me shooting at Mac. I told the police that Mac shot at me and I shot back" "I'm in here for a minute so go holler at that preacher man for me" The guys made the preacher move off the block that same night. I sat in jail for two weeks. My BM told me that she was about to have the baby in a month or so. I told her to tell my mom to sell my car so I can see my son born. I had $500 on my books; all I needed was another $1500. I told my mom to sell my car for $1500; she sold it within a couple of days. It was worth very more than $1500 tho'. I told my mom to give the money to Tez sister Tasha so she can come bond me out. I did not trust their ass holding my money; I would have never got out. My mom only gave her $1150. Instead of them coming to get me out, my mom gave my brothers guy Maine $350. Tasha had to hustle up the missing $350. I had to stay locked up for a couple more weeks. Tasha finally came and bonded me out. I went over to her house for a while, and then I walked from 12th to 5th street, feeling good that I was free. I walked through the gangway of the Apartments where I was staying at the time I shot at Mac. All of the neighbors that witnessed the shooting were looking at me like they saw a ghost. One of them pulled her kid back, like I was a monster. Even my mom acted as if she just saw a ghost, like I was never getting out. I walked up the street; she had fags sitting in the front yard playing cards. I heard while I was locked up, Maine was fucking Brah's BM. I walked in the house and snapped. I see Maine and then I seen Brah's BM lying in my bed. I said, "Fat bitch, get up and get the fuck out! Maine you get the fuck out too! My mom told me "you just don't show up at home telling people to get out of my house" I said to her "bitch this is my house. I got this house for us and you letting this mothafucka fuck Brah's BM in our house. What the fuck happened to the rest of my money that you sold my car for? She said, "I gave it to Maine so he can get right!" I asked him "what's good with my money and my puppy" he told me he was broke and somebody broke into his house and stole my dog. He tried to get tough. I told him "step outside. I'm gon beat yo ass!" He would not step outside. I told him "get the fuck out my house! And take these fags with you" Tasha gave me $200 to get back on my feet and it did not take me long. Later on the night…Vodka found out I was out of jail. She showed up at my back door in the middle of the night. She was wearing a long coat with panties and a bra under it…

Choked Out

My BM and I were into it when I got out. I heard that she was fucking my guy 444 while I was locked up. I did not talk to her until she was in the hospital. Her aunt called me and told me "Sheena is in the hospital, she didn't want you up here because you told her that the baby wasn't yours" I got up to the hospital and her auntie was staring me up and down. This bitch just moved here from Mississippi, she does not even know me, and she did not like me. My BM had the baby and I told her what I wanted to name my son. As soon as the doctor came back in the room and asked my BM, "do you have a name for him yet?" This bitch turns to her Auntie that just came from Mississippi and let her name my son! That pissed me off! I had to leave out the hospital. I was about to snap. I went back up to the hospital the next day and she was gone. I am running around town looking for her and my son. It has been 3 days since I saw my son. I go by her auntie's house and she told me; that she did not want me to see him, because I asked was he my son. I was mad because she let her auntie name my son. A couple days later, my BM brought him to her mom's house and her friends came over to see him. My BM and I were arguing. Four of her friends were about to come in the house, 444's sister, her friend, a fag, and his sister. 444's sister and her friend said "I see that y'all are having some problems, we'll just gonna come back later" As they were walking out the fag and his sister looked me up and down and walked right past me. The fag went in the bathroom, while I was trying to talk. I was telling them "this not a good time, I'm already mad!" The Little gay-gay and his sister were trying to test me. I asked them to leave; now this bitch gets jazzy with me. I snapped. I grabbed the bitch by the throat and choked her out. I mean, she fall straight to sleep! Ha. The Little gay-gay came out of the bathroom; sees his sister passed out on the ground, he goes straight to the kitchen, and start to throw dishes at me. He was yelling at his sister "wake up! Wake up, bitch please!" My BM's little sister ran into the bathroom with the phone. I heard her talking to the police. I bent over and ripped the phone cord out the wall. My BM's sister was saying, "Pig, just leave, just leave!" The fag was yelling "wake up, Nia. Pass me my mace out my coat," I said "mother fucka if you spray the mace in this house, I ma kill you, bitch!" I called my guy Bull, and told him to bring my gun to my BM's back door. Got Damn--All of a sudden, I feel this throbbing pain on the back of my neck. This fucking fag hit me on the back of my neck with a skillet. I heard some loud banging on the door front door. I had told Bull to come to the back door. I thought to myself… I already know who this is. I look down the stairs and it is the police. My BM's sister dialed 911, but since I disconnected her call, they came anyways. I went down the stairs to open the door for them and they said "not you again Mr. Jackson. I told you, "you're not even supposed to be over here" While I'm talking to them, they're putting the handcuffs on me and I say to them "y'all aren't even trying to hear my side of the story before you put these cuffs on me". The gay-gay's sister finally woke up and came running down the stairs. She screamed to the police "he choked me out, he put me to sleep, and I want him locked up!" The police said, "That's all we needed to hear" They locked me up.

3 BALLS

All I could think about was how my bond was going to be revoked. When I got to the County, I forgot all about I had three balls on me! As the sheriff was searching me, I am talking to him and let him know about everything that had just happened to me. I saw the three balls fall on the ground, so I covered them up with my foot. I scooted them over to the trashcan. While, trying to distract the sheriff, I asked him if there was a big knot on the back of my neck, from being hit with a skillet. As he looked at my neck, I kicked the three balls under the trashcan. The sheriff told me to step to my right, and I went into the holding cell. *God Has Plans For Me.* I spent one night in jail, they did not come press charges on me, so they let me go! I went back over to my BM crib; they called my BM and told her to tell me that their BROTHER IS ABOUT TO KILL ME! I got both of my vests, for me and my guy Bull. I grabbed my snub nose 38, Bull grabbed his 9. I told my BM to tell them "they brother know where I am at!" Those bitches never came around. It got hot as hell outside and the vest had me sweating like a mother fucka, I went and took it off. They knew what it was! A few hours later my BM's auntie, from Mississippi came to her house. Her auntie and I started arguing. She called the police on me and I did not even know it until they pulled up. I had the snub nose on my hip. I told the police officer to hold on real quick, I had to run upstairs. They let me go! Once I got up there, I ran out the back door. *God has plans for me* When I got up the alley, a car was driving past. It was someone I did not really know, but she knew me. I jumped in her backseat, lay down, and thought to myself "Damn, I left my vest!" I asked her to take me to my house. (I stayed on 5th street) A few minutes later, my BM's little sister called me. She told me that her auntie threw the vest over the balcony, to the police and they were looking for it. I stayed away from my BM for a minute.

Chaos; disorganized

It was time to get back to the money! My new hangout spot was Enterprise. I been out for about two months now, I finally got my money back up. I could afford to give some of the guys double ups. There was this one new guy name Chaos. He had just moved into the building. I had been serving him double ups for a while now. Then one of the guys came to me and told me that Chaos was smoking on that shit. I had to cut him off! I started supplying him like one my cluckers. But I gave him a little extra to make him feel special. He came to me one day and said "man, I only made my money back off the last one you gave me" I just had to tell him "man, stop smoking that shit and you will see your profit" He tried to deny that he was smoking, I just walked off. The next day I came over and one of my clucks walked up. Chaos had the nerve to tell me "next time one of your people comes, you have to serve them in the alley" (that is when I really knew he was on that shit) But, I gave him a pass that day. I was 17 at the time; he was like, in his 30s. But, he did not know whom he was fucking with and this was not what he wanted. I gave him a pass and told him to move around with that bullshit! Then everybody in the building gave him a warning, telling him "man, you better leave Pig alone, now" After that, every time I came over, I was making sure he did not make any money in the building. Now, the shit that I sold him before, I made him sit on it, until I would leave the spot and go home. I guess he built his courage up and came to me. Everybody warned him. He came to me again. He said, "Man, I told you, when yo people come, you have to take them to the alley and serve them!" I told him "man, why are you fucking with me? THIS AINT WHAT YOU WANT! You need to leave me the fuck alone!" As I was walking out the gate he said "how you out here flipping ounces and yo brother locked up? Nigga you the police." He tried to throw salt on my name. Everybody out there knew I did not like the police and he pissed me off when he mentioned my brother. I am about to beat his ass! I moved towards him and jumped up the stairs; I twisted my ankle and almost fell. When I stumbled towards him, he thought I was about to hit him, so he flinched. He saw that everybody seen his bitch-ness, when he flinched. He ran up on me; I hit him with a two-piece, so quick, put him straight to sleep, he fell right into my arms… (To remind you, it had been a year since I have had to whoop somebodies ass) My ankle was hurting so bad, that I had to drag him and lean my back up against the house to continue whooping his ass. While holding his hair, I hit him one more time to wake him up. I am talking to him "I told you this ain't with you want" so I knock him out again! Every time I hit him; his bitch screamed at the top of her lungs "please don't hit him no more, Pig" so I hit him again to wake him up. I talked to him again, and then knocked him out one last time. I threw him down, his head bounced off the concrete, and that woke him up. While I was walking away, he got up, and stumbled up the stairs. He stood on the porch and started to throw bottles at me "straight bitch move" I told him "you throw another bottle at me, I'm gon come back and blow yo shit off ". He took his bitch ass in the crib. I went home. That next morning, I went over to the spot and there was a big ass burn spot on the porch! I asked everybody what happened. They told me, that Chaos told them, that I came back over to the house last night and tried to burn the house down! I asked everybody "do y'all really think that I would do some shit like this" My guy Donnie just had a baby and my guy little C's mom stayed in the building. Donnie's cousin told me that Chaos was trying to get a gun from him. He tried to frame me with a fire to turn my people against me. This Bitch Ass Nigga tried to pull "the divide and conquer". So I personally walked up to his apartment and told him "you just tried to burn down the spot, and blame me. Nigga, you have to move outta here!" He moved back to Bloomington the next day!!

Bibliography

Bonczar, T. *Prevalence of Imprisonment in the US Population* 1974-2001. Washington D.C. Bureau of Justice Statistics. Online

http://www.sentencingproject.org/template/index.cfm

Brown, Les

http://freewebcoach.org/les-brown-live-full-and-die-empty-quotes-and-video/

Gates, Kevin

http://www.azlyrics.com/lyrics/kevingates/getuponmylevel.html

http://www.azlyrics.com/lyrics/kevingates/again.html

Gotti, Yo

http://genius.com/2830795/Yo-gotti-cold-blood/That-created-the-hunger-and-that-make-the-monsters

Hill, Napoleon

http://www.goodreads.com/quotes/77253-whatever-the-mind-can-conceive-and-believe-it-can-achieve

Kang, Taewoon, Kaye, H. Stephen, and LaPlante, Mitchell P

http://dsc.ucsf.edu/publication.php

Lincoln, Abraham.

http://www.abrahamlincolnonline.org/lincoln/speeches/fair.htm

Thomas, Eric

http://www.etquotes.com/quotes/pain-is-temporary-it-may-last-for-a-minute-or-an-hour-or-a-day-or-even-a-year-but-eventually-it-will-subside-and-something-else-take-its-place-if-i-quit-however-it-will-last-forever/

Trip, Don

http://genius.com/Don-trip-letter-to-my-son-lyrics

Waldo, Ralph Emerson.

http://www.goodreads.com/quotes/313402-treat-a-man-as-he-is-and-he-will-remain

To be continued in Vol II